Interpretations of the Shrimad Bhagwat Gita

MAMTA MEHROTRA

PRABHAT
PRAKASHAN

Published by
PRABHAT PRAKASHAN PVT. LTD.
4/19 Asaf Ali Road,
New Delhi-110002 (INDIA)
e-mail: prabhatbooks@gmail.com

ISBN 978-81-961590-8-5
INTERPRETATIONS OF THE SHRIMAD BHAGWAT GITA
by Mamta Mehrotra

Edition
First, 2023

Price
₹ 300 (Rupees Three Hundred Only)

Printed at
Japan Art, Delhi

Blessings from heaven above

Mrs Meena Khanna

Author's Note

The relationship between a Guru and a Shishya is a sacred bond based on mutual respect, trust, and a shared commitment to learn and grow. The teacher transmits knowledge, skills, and values to the student. The teacher is responsible for creating a positive and supportive learning environment that encourages students to engage with the subject matter and develop their own abilities.

At the same time, the relationship between a Guru and a Shishya can also involve elements of mentorship, guidance, and support. Teachers may take on a role as trusted advisors, helping students navigate school challenges and providing advice and encouragement as needed.

Thus, the relationship between a Guru and a Shishya is a dynamic and evolving relationship that can have a profound impact on the lives of both teachers and students, shaping their experiences and futures.

The Gurukul Parampara, the education system of ancient times, emphasises a holistic approach to education, where the emphasis is on not just academic learning but also on physical, emotional, and spiritual development. Students learn not only from textbooks but also from their surroundings and life experiences.

Unfortunately, unlike ancient times when education had a holistic approach, now education has become commercial and money-oriented. From Guru to Shishya, everyone is seeking education to make money out of it. Lost are the traditions, the value system, and the orientation in education. It is time that educationists and academicians reflect upon it and reorient and revamp our education system.

The book, sheds light on the difference between the ancient times' education system and the present times' education system. Moreover, the book expounds on the ways through which the quality of education could be refined. Many interpretations in this book have been taken from 'The Gita' by Swami Chinmayananda ji with few changes made to the language in some chapters to maintain the continuity and the readability for better understanding of the texts. To fully grasp the teaching of 'The Gita', one should follow the deliberations present in 'The Gita' by Swami Chinmayananda Saraswati ji.

Hopefully, the book would help you understand the relationship between a Guru and a Shishya in finer detail and what measures we should take to provide a better learning environment for our young generation.

– Mamta Mehrotra

❑

Contents

General Introduction to the Bhagwat Gita

If the Upanishads are the textbooks of philosophical principles discussing man, world and God, the Gita is a handbook of instructions as to how every human being can come to live the subtle philosophical principles of Vedanta in the actual work-a-day world.

Shrimad Bhagwat Gita, the Divine Song of the Lord, occurs in the Bhishma Parva of the Mahabharata, and comprises eighteen chapters, from the 25th to the 42nd. This great handbook of practical living marked a positive revolution in Hinduism and inaugurated a Hindu renaissance for the ages that followed the Puranic Era.

In the Song of the Lord, the Gita, the Poet-Seer Vyasa has brought the Vedic truths from the sequestered Himalayan caves into the active fields of political life and into the confusing tensions of an imminent fratricidal war. Under the stress of some psychological maladjustments, Arjuna got shattered in his mental equipoise and lost his capacity to act with true discrimination. Lord Krishna takes in hand that neurotic mind of Arjuna for a Hindu treatment with Vedic truths.

Religion is philosophy in action. From time to time an ancient philosophy needs intelligent reinterpretation in the context of new times, and men of wisdom, prophets, and seers guide the common man on how to apply effectively the ancient laws in his present life.

If we try to digest properly the implications of the Gita's advice in the light of 1 dc lore, it becomes amply clear how actions performed without egocentric desires purge the mind of its deep-seated impressions and make it increasingly subtle in its purification and preparation for greater flights into the Infinite Beyond. To explain this, we will just try to review a little the conception of the mind and its functions in our day-to-day life.

Mind is man. As the mind, so is the individual. If the mind is disturbed, the individual is disturbed. If the mind is good, the individual is good. This mind, for purposes of our study and understanding, may be considered as constituted of two distinct sides one facing the world of stimuli that reach it from the objects of the world, and the other facing the 'within' which reacts to the stimuli received. The outer mind facing the object is called the objective mind; in Sanskrit we call it the Manas, and the inner mind is called the subjective mind; in Sanskrit, the Buddhi.

That individual is whole and healthy in whom the objective and subjective aspects of the mind work in unison, and in moments of doubt, the objective mind readily comes under the disciplining influence of the subjective mind. But unfortunately, except for a rare few, the majority of us have minds that are split. This split between the subjective and the objective aspects of our mind is mainly created by the layer of egoistic desires in the individual. The greater the distance between these two aspects of the mind, the greater the inner confusion in the individual, and the greater the egoism and low desires which the individual comes to exhibit in life.

Through the five 'gateways of knowledge', the organs of perception, all of us experience the world of objects around us at all moments of our waking state. The innumerable stimuli that react with our sense organs (receptors), create impulses which reach the objective mind and these impulses filter deep down to the subjective stratum through the intervening layers of individual egocentric desires. These impulses, thus reaching the subjective of a person, react with the existing impressions of his own past actions that are carefully stored away in the subjective layer and express themselves in the world outside through the five organs of action (effectors).

At each moment, man meets with different patterns of these stimuli, and thus constantly gathers new impressions in the 'subjective mind'. Every set of impulses reaching it not only adds to the existing layers of impressions already in it, but also gets coloured by the quality of these vasanas hoarded within. When they are translated into action, the actions carry a flavour of the existing vasanas in the 'subjective mind'.

All of us live constantly meeting a variety of experiences; and at each incident, we perceive, react with the perceived, and come to act in the outer field. In this process, we unwittingly come to hoard in ourselves more and more dirt of new impressions. The 'subjective mind' gets increasingly granulated by overlapping signatures of our past moments. These granulations make the 'subjective mind' dull and opaque, and form, as it were, an impregnable wall between ourselves and the spiritual Divinity that shines eternally as pure consciousness in all of us deep within the core of our personality.

The theory of Vedanta repeats that reduction of the vasanas is the means of volatalising the mind. When I look into a mirror and do not see my face in it, it is not because the mirror is not reflecting the object in front of it, but because the reflected image is not perceptible to my vision due to, perhaps, the thick layer of dust on the mirror. With a duster, when I clean the mirror, the act of cleaning does not create the reflection of the face, but it only unveils the reflection which was already there. Similarly, man is not aware today of his divine spiritual nature because the 'subjective mind' reflecting it is thickly coated with dull vasanas gathered by it during its egocentric, passionate existence in the world.

To bring the subjective and the objective aspects of the mind together into a happy marriage where the 'objective mind' is well-disciplined to act faithfully as per the guidance of the 'subjective', is the Yoga pointed out in the Gita. This is accomplished only by the removal of the dividing factor—the egocentric desires. The typical word used in the Gita to indicate this practical implication of Yoga is self-explanatory—Buddhi Yoga.

When this happy marriage between the subjective and the objective aspects of the mind has taken place, thereafter that equanimous Yogi becomes skilled in action, and he, with his 'objective mind', reacts intelligently and faithfully to the external stimuli; his actions become, as it were, a purgation of the already existing vasanas in his 'subjective mind'. Thus, through intelligent action, an individual can exhaust his existing impressions and ultimately redeem his 'subjective mind' from the granulations and make it more clear and crystalline.

This idea has been emphasised by great commentators like Shankara, who tirelessly repeat that selfless activity, performed in a spirit of egoless adoration and reverence to the divine ideal, would ultimately result in inner purification. This, according to Shankara, is the most unavoidable prerequisite before the subjective mind' can turn inward seeking to rediscover the sanctuary of the Self, the Spiritual Reality.

Spiritually viewed, the 'subjective mind' is thus a secret weapon to be used as an outlet for the existing impressions that have come to be stored up in it. But the tragedy is that an average man, in his ignorance, misuses this dangerous weapon and brings about his own annihilation. He uses it as an INLET and creates, during his selfish activities performed with low motives, a new stock of mental impressions.

In order to exhaust them, nature provides new equipments (bodies), in which the same ego comes to live, repeatedly, life after life. The message of the Gita clearly points out that actions are not to be avoided and the world-of-objects is not to be denied.

On the contrary, by making use of them intelligently, we must strive selflessly, and force the very samsara to provide us with a field for exhausting our mental dirt.

An unhealthy mind divided in itself, as we explained earlier, becomes an easy prey to a host of psychological diseases. Weakened in its constitution, it easily becomes a victim to all contagions. Arjuna was an average educated man, and from the details of the Mahabharata, we know the environments in which he grew up. But for the entire Mahabharata, we would not appreciate so fully Arjuna's mental condition, without which Krishna's message would have fallen flat upon the readers.

Therefore, the Gita is an intrinsic part of the entire Mahabharata and the classic would have been a hotchpotch story, without pith and dignity, if Srimad Bhagwat Gita was not in it—and the Gita would have been a mere philosopher's riddle-poem without the Mahabharata background. The story and the poem together are an organic whole; each devoid of the other would be ineffectual and empty.

Modern psychology exhausts volumes, in describing to us the dreary results of suppression and repression of emotions. There are many moments in our lives when we knowingly suppress many of our emotions; but more often in our day-to-day life, we, unconsciously, repress many of our sentiments. Repressed emotions accumulate a tremendous amount of dynamic energy which must necessarily seek a field for expression. Unless these energies are properly guided they would boomerang back to destroy the very individual. Though there are no direct explanations of any repressions of emotion in Arjuna, a careful student of the story can easily diagnose that the great hero on the battlefield came under the influence of his repressed conditions and behaved as a victim of perfect neurosis.

The causes for his emotional repressions are not far to seek. A great hero, confident of his own strength, was made to live amidst the unjust tyranny of his Machiavellian cousins. At the same time, the great archer could not give vent to his nature because of the righteous policy of peace at all costs' of his eldest brother, Yudhishthira. These repressed emotions found a healthy field for expression in the severe tapas which he performed during his life in the jungles.

During the last year of their lives incognito, the Pandava family had to serve as menials in the palace of the Raja of Virata. The carping injustice and the cruel indignities of the situation caused, no doubt, a lot of repression in Arjuna's mind. But even these found a healthy field of expression in the battle that he had to wage against Duryodhana's forces that came to challenge the Virata might.

After their long and strenuous trials, when the Pandavas at last reached their native kingdom, their tyrant cousin, with no rhyme or reason, denied them not only their right to half of the kingdom, but also all terms of conciliation.

The shrewd, blind Dhritarashtra, father of the Kauravas, probably understood the psychological condition of the great warrior, Arjuna. Hence on the day previous to the great war, he sent Sanjaya, his emissary, to Arjuna with a secret message. This message, full of mischievous import, sowed the seeds of dangerous ideas in the mind of Arjuna, directing his repressed energies into wrong channels, so that he became a hapless neurotic in the face of the great challenge. When we read the chapters of Gita we see that very same arguments and ideas repeated faithfully by Arjuna from the message he had received the previous day from his uncle.

On that fateful day when both the armies were getting into formation, Arjuna asks his charioteer, Lord Krishna, to drive the chariot to a point between the two forces, so that he may review the enemy lines. Larger in number, better equipped, more liberal in supplies and commanded by well-known personalities, the Kaurava formation, expanding itself like an eagle stood poised to swoop down upon the smaller army of the Pandavas. This was a sight severely challenging the mental stamina of the Pandava hero. His 'objective mind' under the impact of the stimuli, could not find any reaction from its 'subjective mind' (Buddhi), because the shattering of these two aspects was complete due to the intervening layers of his egocentric assumptions and desire-prompted anxieties. The dynamic forces released in his mind due to the repressions were not properly channelised, but were misdirected by the suggestions of Dhritarashtra's words, and therefore, the greatest hero of the times, Arjuna, suddenly became a despondent, bewildered, neurotic patient.

The 'Krishna-treatment' of this patient of psychological derangement was certainly a specific cure, inasmuch as, in the last chapter we definitely hear Arjuna declaring that all his 'delusions have ended'. The rest of the story of how, having come into his own, he became a rejuvenated warrior of tremendous strength and valour, is quite well-known to all students of this great classic.

In varying degrees, every man is a victim of this 'Arjuna-Disease' and the 'Krishna-Cure' being specific, is available to all of us at all times in the philosophy of the Gita.

In the Second Chapter, which is almost a summary of the entire Gita, Krishna indicates the two main lines of treatment. One is a 'treatment of Idealism' wherein Arjuna is directed to a greater Reality than his mind, ego and intellect and thereby the divorce between the 'subjective' and the 'objective' aspects of his mind is eliminated to some extent. In the second half of the same chapter, we shall read and come to understand how selfless activity will purge the existing vasanas in the individual. Arjuna being a Kshatriya, his mind was coloured by the impression of Rajo-guna (activity), and so he needed a battlefield to exhaust those impressions.

Thus, we find Krishna repeatedly goading his friend with the words, "Get up and fight". This need not necessarily mean that the Gita is a war-mongering scripture of the ruling-class. It is a call to each one of us to get up and fight the battle of our own life, according to our own vasanas (Swadharma), so that we may exhaust them and thus gain inner purity. As we take it up stanza by stanza, for a close study of the entire Song, we shall try to see how Krishna indicates the same truth from different angles of vision and explains it in different words.

As an excerpt taken from the writings of Swami Chinmayananda ji. His interpretation of this text guided me to revisit this text and understand it as a cure for the mental illness engulfing all of us.

OM OM OM

Arjuna-Grief

Introduction

No other race in the world had ever harnessed so successfully the scintillating possibilities of the drama in literature for the purposes of philosophical exposition as the ancient Hindus. The Upanishads were recorded in the form of conversations between the teacher and the taught, in the quiet atmosphere of the silent and peaceful Himalayan valleys. In the Gita, however, the highest and the best in Hindu philosophy have been reiterated, in a more elaborate and detailed dramatic layout amidst the din and roar of a total—war. Krishna gives his message of manly-action to Arjuna amidst the breathing, palpitating environment of the clash and carnage of a battlefield.

The Kauravas, hundred in number, represent the innumerable ungodly forces of negative tendencies within man's bosom, and the Pandavas, no doubt, represent the divine impulses in him. A constant Mahabharata war is being waged within every one of us at all our crucial moments of action; and in all cases, the negative forces in each one of us are larger in number and usually mightier in their effectiveness, while the inner divine army is ever lesser in number and apparently, comparatively weaker in efficiency. Therefore, every single individual, at the moment of his inward checking up, must necessarily feel the desperations of Arjuna.

The story of the Mahabharata sounds an optimistic note of hope to man that, even though the diviner impulses are seemingly less in number, if the same are organised fully and brought under the guidance of the Supreme Lord, Krishna, the Self; then, under His guidance, they can easily be ushered into a true and permanent victory over the outnumbering forces of lust and greed.

The Kauravas, representing the negative tendencies and the sinful motives in a mortal's bosom, are born as children to the old king, Dhritarashtra, a born-blind prince. He was wedded to Gandhari, who had voluntarily blinded herself by putting bandages over her eyes! Commentators are tempted to see in this, a very appropriate significance. Mind is born-blind to truth, and when it is wedded to an intellect, which has also assumed blindness, the negative instincts yoked with low motives can only beget a hundred criminalities and sins!

When, upon the spiritual field of self-development within (Dharmakshetra), the lower instincts and the higher ideals array themselves, ready to fight, a true seeker (the captain of the latter), under the guidance of his divine discriminative intellect, takes himself to a point on no-man's land between the two forces for the purpose of reviewing the enemy lines, without identifying himself with either the good or the evil in him. At that moment of his introspective meditations, the egoistic entity comes to feel a morbid desperation and feels generally incapacitated to undertake the great spiritual adventure of fighting his inner war with any hope of victory.

This peculiar mental condition of a seeker is beautifully represented in the vivid picture of Arjuna's dejection in the opening chapter.

In Sanskrit works, it is a recognised tradition that the opening stanza should generally indicate the whole theme of the text. The bulk of the book, then discusses at length, the different views and gives all possible arguments, until in its concluding portion, the last stanza generally summarises the final conclusions of the shastra on the theme indicated in the opening section of the book. In this way, when we consider the Gita, we find that the Divine

Song starts with the word 'Dharma' and concludes with the term 'Mine' (Mama); and therefore, the contents of the Gita—we may conclude—are nothing but 'My Dharma' (Mama Dharma).

The term Dharma is one of the most intractable terms in Hindu philosophy. Derived from the root 'dhar' (Dhri) to uphold, sustain, support, the term Dharma denotes "that which holds together the different aspects and qualities of an object into a whole". Ordinarily, the term Dharma has been translated as religious code, as righteousness, as a system of morality, as duty, as charity, etc. But the original Sanskrit term has a special connotation of its own which is not captured by any one of these renderings. The best rendering of this term Dharma that I have met with so far is, the law-of-Being meaning, "that which makes a thing or being what it is". For example, it is the Dharma of the Fire to burn, of the Sun to shine, etc.

Dharma means, therefore, not merely righteousness or goodness but it indicates the essential nature of anything, without which it cannot retain its independent existence.

For example, a cold, dark Sun is impossible, as heat and light are the Dharma of the Sun. Similarly, if we are to live truly dynamic men in the world, we can only do so by being faithful to our true nature, and the Gita explains to me 'my Dharma'.

In using thus the first person possessive noun, this scripture perhaps indicates that the Song, Divine sung through the eighteen chapters is to be subjectively transcribed, lived, and personally experienced by each student in his own life.

Dhritarashtra said:

1. What did the sons of Pandu and also my people do, when, desirous to fight, they assembled together on the holy plain of Kurukshetra, O Sanjaya?

In the entire Gita, this is the only verse which the blind old king Dhritarashtra gives out. All the rest of the seven hundred stanzas are Sanjaya's report on what happened on the Kurukshetra battlefield, just before the war.

The blind old king is certainly conscious of the palpable injustices that he had done to his nephews, the Pandavas.

धृतराष्ट्र उवाच—

धर्मक्षेत्रे कुरुक्षेत्रे समवेता युयुत्सवः ।

मामकाः पाण्डवाश्चैव किमकुर्वत सञ्जय ॥ १ ॥

dhritarastra uvacha
dharmakşhetre kurukshetre samaveta yuyutsavah
mamakāḥ pandavāśchaiva kimakurvata sañjaya 1.

Dhritarashtra knew the relative strength of the two armies, and therefore, was fully confident of the larger strength of his son's army. And yet, the viciousness of his past and the consciousness of the crimes perpetrated seem to be weighing heavily upon the heart of the blind king, and so he has his own doubts on the outcome of this war. He asks Sanjaya to explain to him, what is happening on the battlefield of Kurukshetra. Vyasa had given Sanjaya the powers to see and listen to the happenings in far-off Kurukshetra even while he was sitting beside Dhritarashtra in the palace at Hastinapura. It happens with most individuals that their conscious prides bring forth the sins they have committed. When our minds are overshadowed by our vices such as greed, arrogance and revenge, it is then that our sins seem to overpower us.

Sanjaya said:

2. Having seen the army of the Pandavas drawn up in battle array, King Duryodhana then approached his teacher (Drona) the and spoke these words.

From this stanza onwards, we have the report of Sanjaya upon what he saw and heard on the warfront at Kurukshetra. When Duryodhana saw the Pandava-forces arrayed for battle, though they were less in number than his own forces, yet the tyrant felt his self-confidence draining away. As a child would run to its in fright, so too, Duryodhana, unsettled in his mind, runs to his teacher,

Dronacharya. When our motives are impure and our cause unjust, however well equipped we may be, our minds should necessarily feel restless and agitated. This is the mental condition of all tyrants and lusty dictators.

सञ्जय उवाच—

दृष्ट्वा तु पाण्डवानीकं व्यूढं दुर्योधनस्तदा ।
आचार्यमुपसङ्गम्य राजा वचनमब्रवीत् ॥ २ ॥

sanjaya uvaca
dṛṣṭvā tu pāṇḍavānīkaṁ vyudham duryodhanastada
acaryamupasangamya raja vacavamabravit 2.

3. Behold, O Teacher! This mighty army of the sons of Pandu arrayed by the son of Drupada, thy wise disciple.

It is indeed stupid of Duryodhana to point out to Drona the army formation of the Pandavas. Later on also, we shall find Duryodhana talking too much and that is a perfect symptom indicating the inward fears of the great king over the final outcome of the unjust war.

4. Here are heroes, mighty archers, equal in battle to Bhima and Arjuna, Yuyudhana, Virata and Drupada, each commanding eleven-thousand archers,

5. Dhrishtaketu, Chekitana, and the valiant king of Kashi, Purujit and Kuntibhoja and Saibya, the best of men.

पश्यैतां पाण्डुपुत्राणामाचार्य महतीं चमूम् ।
व्यूढां द्रुपदपुत्रेण तव शिष्येण धीमता ॥ ३ ॥

pasyaitam panduputrānāmācārya mahatim camm
vyadham drupadaputrena tava sisyana dhimata 3.

अत्र शूरा महेष्वासा भीमार्जुनसमा युधि ।
युयुधानो विराटश्च द्रुपदश्च महारथः ॥ ४ ॥

atra sura maheṣvasa bhimarjunasama yudhi
yuyudhano viratasca drupasca maharathaḥ 4.

धृष्टकेतुश्चेकितानः काशिराजश्च वीर्यवान् ।
पुरुजित्कुन्तिभोजश्च शैब्यश्च नरपुङ्गवः ॥ ५ ॥

dhrstaketuścekitanah kaširajašca viryavananth
purujitkuntibhojasya saibyaśca narapungavah 5.

6. The strong Yudhamanyu and the brave Uttamaujas, the son of Subhadra and the sons of Draupadi, all of them, divisional commanders.

In these three stanzas, we have a list of names of all those who were noted personalities in the Pandava army. Duryodhana, reviewing his enemies standing in formation, recognises very many noted men of war functioning as maharathas in the Pandava forces. A maharathi was in charge of a group of 11,000 archers, which formed a division in the ancient Hindu army.

Arjuna and Bhima were accepted men of war, noted for archery and strength. These enumerated heroes were, says Duryodhana, each as great as Arjuna and Bhima, the implication being that though the Pandava forces were less in number, their total effectiveness was much greater than that of the larger and better equipped army of the Kauravas, to platom author

7. Know also, O best among the twice-born, the names of those who are the most distinguished amongst ourselves, the leaders of my army; these I name to thee for thy information.

युधामन्युश्च विक्रान्त उत्तमौजाश्च वीर्यवान् ।
सौभद्रो द्रौपदेयाश्च सर्व एव महारथाः ॥ ६ ॥

yudhamanyusca vikranta uttamaujaśca viryavan
saubhadro dropadeyasca sarva eva maharathaḥ 6.

अस्माकं तु विशिष्टा ये तान्नि बोध द्विजोत्तम ।
नायका मम सैन्यस्य संज्ञार्थं तान्ब्रवीमि ते ॥ ७ ॥

asmakam tu visista ye tannibodha dvijottama
nayaka mama sainyasa sanjñārtha tänbravimi te 7.

Addressing his master as 'the best among the twice-born', Duryodhana now repeats the names of the distinguished heroes in his own army. A weak man, to escape from his own mental fears, will whistle to himself in the dark. The guilty conscience of the tyrant king had undermined all his mental strength. The more he realised the combined strength of the great personalities arrayed in the opposite enemy camp, the more abjectly nervous he felt, in spite of the fact that his own army was also manned by highly competent heroes. In order to revive himself, he wanted to hear words of encouragement from his teachers and elders. But when Duryodhana met Drona, the Aacharya chose to remain silent and the helpless king had to find for himself new means of encouragement to revive his own drooping enthusiasm. Therefore, he started enumerating the great leaders in his own army.

When a person has thus, completely lost his morale due to the heavy burden of his own crimes weighing on his conscience, it is but natural that he loses all sense of proportion in his words. At such moments of high tension, an individual clearly exhibits his true mental culture. He addresses his own teacher as 'the best among the twice-born'.

A Brahmana is considered as 'twice-born' because of his inner spiritual development. When born from his mother's womb man comes into the world only as the animal called man. Thereafter, through study and contemplation, he gains more and more discipline, and a cultured Hindu is called a Brahmana (Brahmin).

After all, Drona is a Brahmana by birth and as such, he must have a greater share of softness of heart. Moreover, the enemy lines are fully manned by his own dear students. As a shrewd dictator, Duryodhana entertained shameless doubts about the loyalty of his own teacher.

This is but an instinctive fear, which is natural with all men of foul motives and crooked dealings. When we are not ourselves pure, we will project our own weaknesses and impurities on others who are working around us as our subordinates.

8. Yourself and Bhishma, and Karna and also Kripa, the victorious in war; Aswatthama, Vikarna, and so also the son of Somadatta.

Though Duryodhana, in his mental hysteria, got slightly upset at the subjective onslaught of his own brutal motives and past crimes, like the true dictator that he was, he regained his balance in no time. The moment he had spilt out in his insulting arrogance, the term 'twice-born' in addressing his teacher, he realised that he had overstepped the bounds of discretion. Perhaps the cold silence of the revered Acharya spoke amply to Duryodhana.

भवान्भीष्मश्च कर्णश्च कृपश्च समितिञ्जयः ।
अश्वत्थामा विकर्णश्च सौमदत्तिस्तथैव च ॥ ८ ॥

bhavanbhişmasca karnaśca krpasca samitiñjayah
asvatthämä vikarṇasca saumadattistathaiva cha 8.

9. And many other heroes also who are determined to give up their lives for my sake, armed with various weapons and missiles, all well-skilled in battle.

The incorrigible vanity of the dictatorial tyrant is amply clear when he arrogates to himself the stupendous honour that such a vast array of heroes had come ready to lay down their lives for 'MY SAKE'. To all careful students of the Mahabharata, it cannot be very difficult to estimate how many of these great veterans would have thrown in their lot with Duryodhana, had it not been for the fact that Bhishma, the grandsire, was fighting in the ranks of the Kauravas.

10. This army of ours defended by Bhishma is insufficient, whereas that army of theirs defended by Bhima is sufficient. Or, this army of ours protected by Bhishma is unlimited, whereas that army of theirs protected by Bhima is limited.

In the art of warfare, then known among the ancient Hindus, each army had, no doubt, a commander-in-chief, but it also had a powerful man of valour, courage and intelligence, who functioned as the 'defender'. In the Kaurava forces, Bhishma officiated as the 'defender', and in the Pandava forces, Bhima held the office.

अन्ये च बहवः शूरा मदर्थे त्यक्तजीविताः ।
नानाशस्त्रप्रहरणाः सर्वे युद्धविशारदाः ॥ ९ ॥

anye ca bahavaḥ sura madartha tyaktajivitaḥ
nanāsastraprharaṇaḥ sarve yuddhavisaradaḥ 9.

अपर्याप्तं तदस्माकं बलं भीष्माभिरक्षितम् ।
पर्याप्तं त्विदमेतेषां बलं भीमाभिरक्षितम् ॥ १० ॥

apayārptaṁ tadasmākaṁ balam bhiṣmabhiraksitam
payārptaṁ tvidameteṣāṁ balam bhimabhirakṣitam 10

11. Therefore do you all, stationed in your respective positions in the several divisions of the army, protect Bhishma alone.

After thus expressing in a soliloquy, his own estimate of the relative strength and merit of the two forces, now arrayed, ready for a total war, the king in Duryodhana rises above his mental clouds of desperation to shoot forth his imperial orders to his army officers. He advises them that each commander must keep to his position and fight in disciplined order, and all of them should spare no pains to see that the revered Bhishma is well protected. Perhaps, Duryodhana suspects that the lusty force that he had mobilised is an ill-assorted heterogeneous army constituted of the various tribal chieftains and kings of distant lands and that the strength of such an army could be assured, only when they hold on to a united strategy in all their various manoeuvres. Synchronisation of the different operations is the very backbone of an army's success, and in order to bring this about, as a true strategist, Duryodhana is instructing his various commanders working in different wings to work out the single policy of protecting Bhishma.

अयनेषु च सर्वेषु यथाभागमवस्थिताः ।
भीष्ममेवाभिरक्षन्तु भवन्तः सर्व एव हि ॥ ११ ॥

ayaneşu ca sarveşu yathabhagamavasthitaḥ
bhişmamevābhirakṣantu bhavantuḥ sarva eva hi 11.

12. His glorious grandsire (Bhishma), the oldest of the Kauravas, in order to cheer Duryodhana, now sounded aloud a lion's Tour and blew his conch.

All the while, that Duryodhana was busy making a fool of himself and in his excitement putting all the great officers of his army into an uncomfortable mood of desperate unhappiness, Bhishma was standing, not too far away, observing the pitiable confusions of the tyrant. The revered grandsire noticed, intelligently, in Dronacharya's silence, the outraged temper of a man of knowledge and action. He realised that the situation could be saved only if all those assembled were jerked out of their mental preoccupations. The more they were let alone with their revolting thoughts against Duryodhana, the more they would become ineffectual for the imminent battle. Understanding this psychology of the officers under his command, the great Marshall, Bhishma took up his war-bugle (conch) and blew it, sending forth roaring waves of confidence into the hearts of the people manning the array.

This action of Bhishma, though performed by him out of pity for Duryodhana's mental condition, amounted to an act of aggression almost corresponding to the 'first-bullet-shot' in modern warfare. With this lion-roar, the Mahabharata war was actually started, and for all historical purposes, the Kauravas had thereby, become the aggressors.

तस्य संजनयन्हर्षं कुरुवृद्धः पितामहः ।
सिंहनादं विनद्योच्चैः शङ्खं दध्मौ प्रतापवान् ॥ १२ ॥

tasya sañjanayanharṣam kuruvyddhaḥ pitamahah
simhanadam vinadyoccaiḥ sankham dadhmau pratapavän 12.

13. Then (following Bhishma), conches and kettledrums, tabors, drums and cow-horns blared forth quite suddenly and their sound was tremendous.

All the commanders were, no doubt, in high tension, and as soon as they heard the marshal's bugle, individually, each one of them took up his instrument and sounded the battle-cry. Thus, conches and kettledrums, tabors and trumpets, bugles and cow-horns, all burst forth into a challenging war-call, which Sanjaya, half-heartedly, describes as 'tremendous'. Later on, we shall find that when this challenge was replied to by the Pandavas, the sound was described by Sanjaya as 'terrific', resounding throughout heaven and earth, and rending the hearts of the Kauravas. Here is another instance to prove that Sanjaya was, evidently, a moral objector to the war-aim of Duryodhana. Therefore, we have in him, a most sympathetic reporter of the message of the Lord at the battlefront, as given out in His Song Divine.

14. Then, also Madhava and the son of Pandu, seated in their b ard to magnificent chariot yoked with white horses, blew their divine conches.

ततः शङ्खाश्च भेर्यश्च पणवानकगोमुखाः ।
सहसैवाभ्यहन्यन्त स शब्दस्तुमुलोऽभवत् ॥ १३ ॥

tataḥ sankhaśc bheryasch Opanvanakagomukhah
sahasaivabhyahanyanta sa sabdastumulo'bhavat 13.

ततः श्वेतैर्हयैर्युक्ते महति स्यन्दने स्थितौ ।
माधवः पाण्डवश्चैव दिव्यौ शङ्खौ प्रदध्मतुः ॥ १४ ॥

tatah svetairhayairyukte mahati syandane sthitau
madhavaḥ pandavaścaiva divyau sankhau pradadhmatuh 14.

The wealth of detail that has been so lavishly squandered in expressing a simple fact that, from the Pandava-side, Krishna and Arjuna answered the battle-cry, clearly shows where Sanjaya's sympathies lay. Here, the description—sitting in the magnificent chariot, harnessed with white horses, Madhava and Arjuna blew their conches divine—clearly echoes the hope lurking in the heart of Sanjaya that due to the apparent contrast in the two descriptions; perhaps, even at this moment Dhritarashtra may be persuaded to withdraw his sons from the warfront.

15. Hrishikesha blew the Panchajanya and Dhananjaya (Arjuna) blew the Devadatta and Vrikodara (Bhima), the doer of terrible deeds, blew the great conch, named Paundra.

In his description of the Pandava array, Sanjaya is very particular to mention even the name of each warrior's special conch. Panchajanya was blown by Krishna.

Hrishikesha is the name of the Lord and it has often been described as meaning the "Lord of the Senses". But this is according to an old derivation: Hrishika + Isha = Lord of the Senses. But the word 'Hrishika' is an obscure one. Modern commentators prefer to explain it as Hrish + kasha = Having short hair.

पाञ्चजन्यं हृषीकेशो देवदत्तं धनञ्जयः ।
पौण्ड्रं दध्मौ महाशङ्ख भीमकर्मा वृकोदरः ॥ १५ ॥

pañchajanyam hṛṣikeso devadattam dhananjanyah
paundram dadhmau mahasankham bhimakamār vrkodarah 15,

16. King Yudhisthira, the son of Kunti, blew the Anantavijaya: Nakula and Sahadeva blew the Sughosha and the Manipushpaka.

17. The king of Kashi, an excellent archer, Shikhandi, the mighty commander of eleven thousand archers, Dhristadyumna and Virata and Satyaki, the unconquered;

18. Drupada and the sons of Draupadi, O Lord of the Earth, and the son of Subhadra, the mighty armed, blew their respective conches.

In the above verses, we have the enumeration of the great Maharathas, battalion-commanders, who, with enthusiasm, loudly blew their conches, again and again, in an ascending cadence. The arrow that ultimately felled Bhishma in the Mahabharata-war came from Shikhandi. The charioteer of Krishna, who was also a battalion-commander in the Pandava army, was called Satyaki.

अनन्तविजयं राजा कुन्तीपुत्रो युधिष्ठिरः ।
नकुलः सहदेवश्च सुघोषमणिपुष्पकौ ॥ १६ ॥

anantavijayam raja kuntiputro yudhisthirah
nakulah sahadevasca sughoṣamanipuspakau 16.

काश्यश्च परमेष्वासः शिखण्डी च महारथः ।
धृष्टद्युम्नो विराटश्च सात्यकिश्चापराजितः ॥ १७ ॥

kasyaśca parameṣvasaḥ sikhandi ca maharathah
dhrstadyumno viratasca satyakiścaparajitah 17.

द्रुपदो द्रौपदेयाश्च सर्वशः पृथिवीपते ।
सौभद्रश्च महाबाहुः शङ्खान्दध्मुः पृथक्पृथक् ॥ १८ ॥

drupado draupadeyaśca sarvasaḥ prthivipate
saubhadrasca mahabahuḥ sankhändadhmu pṛthakprthak 18.

The report is being addressed to Dhritarashtra and it is indicated by Sanjaya's words, "Oh Lord of the earth".

19. That tumultuous sound rent the hearts of (the people of) Dhritarashtra's party and made both heaven and earth reverberate.

From the fourteenth stanza onwards, Sanjaya gives us in all detail, an exhaustive description of the Pandava forces, and he spares no pains to bring into the mind of Dhritarashtra a vivid understanding of the superiority of the Pandava forces. Perhaps, the minister hopes that his blind king will realise the disastrous end and, at least now, will send forth a command to stop the fratricidal war.

20-21. Then, seeing the people of Dhritarashtra's party standing by to arrayed and the discharge of weapons about to begin, Arjuna, the son of Pandu, whose ensign was a monkey,X thetook up his bow and said these words to Krishna rin Hrshi (Hrishikesha), O Lord of the Earth!

स घोषो धार्तराष्ट्राणां हृदयानि व्यदारयत् ।
नभश्च पृथिवीं चैव तुमुलो व्यनुनादयन् ॥ १९ ॥

sa ghoso dhartaraṣṭrānām hrdayani vyadarayat
nabhaśca prthiavi caiva tumulo vyanunadayan 19.

अथ व्यवस्थितान्दृष्ट्वा धार्तराष्ट्रान्कपिध्वजः ।
प्रवृत्ते शस्त्रसंपाते धनुरुद्यम्य पाण्डवः ॥ २० ॥

atha vyavasthitandṛṣṭvä dhärtaraṣṭränkapidhwajah
pravṛtte sastra-sampate dhanurudyamya pandavaḥ 20.

हृषीकेशं तदा वाक्यमिदमाह महीपते ।

hṛṣikesam tada vakyamidamah mahipate

In these one and a half verses we have a description of the arrival of the hero of the Mahabharata war, Arjuna, on the battlefield. The exact time and nature of his entry are noted here. The shooting had not yet started, but it was imminent. It was the most tense moment; the crisis had risen to its highest pitch. It was at this moment that Arjuna, whose ensign was that of Hanuman, said the following words to Lord Krishna.

In those ancient days of chivalrous warfare, each honoured hero had his own personal flag, carrying on it conspicuously, and a well-recognised symbol. By the flag flying on the chariot, the enemy could recognise who was the occupant of the chariot. A hero was not generally shot at by an ordinary soldier, but each fought with his equal on the battlefield. This system of carrying a symbol to recognize individuals in the battlefield is faithfully followed even in modern warfare. A high official's vehicle carries insignia of the officer's rank on its very number-plate; on the very uniform enough details are pinned on to recognize the wearer and identify him. Arjuna's ensign was that of a monkey.

The stanza also gives us, in hasty strokes, the information that Arjuna was impatient to start the righteous war. He had raised his instrument of war, his bow, indicating his readiness to fight.

Arjuna said:

21. In the midst of the two armies, place my chariot, O Achyuta.

अर्जुन उवाच —

सेनयोरुभयोर्मध्ये रथं स्थापय मेऽच्युत ॥ २१ ॥

Arjuna uvach
senayorubhayormadhye ratham sthäpaya me'cyuta 21.

22. That I may behold those who stand here desirous of fighting and on the eve of this battle, let me know with whom I must fight.

Here, we hear Arjuna's soldier-like command to his charioteer to drive and place the vehicle between the two armies so that he might see and recognise the various heroes whom he has to meet and fight in the Great War. In expressing thus, a wish to review the enemy lines, the great hero is showing his daring and chivalry, his great courage and firm determination, his adventurous readiness and indomitable energy. Up to this point in the story, Arjuna, the invincible hero of the Mahabharata, was in his own true element unaffected by any mental hysteria.

23. For I desire to observe those who are assembled here for the fight, wishing to please in battle, the evil-minded sons of A ne bewollo linat Dhritarashtra.

The verse only reinforces our impression of Arjuna gathered in the previous lines. He is giving the reason why he wants to review the enemy lines. As a man of action, he did not want to take any undue risk and so wanted to see for himself who were the low-minded, power-mad, greed- ridden men who had joined the forces of the Kauravas, supporting the palpably tyrannical and evidently unjust cause of the unscrupulous Duryodhana.

यावदेतान्निरीक्षेऽहं योद्धुकामानवस्थितान् ।
कैर्मया सह योद्धव्यमस्मिन्रणसमुद्यमे ॥ २२ ॥

yavadetannirikṣe ham yoddhukämänavasthitav
kairmaya saha yoddhavyamasmainranasamudyame 22.

योत्स्यमानानवेक्षेऽहं य एतेऽत्र समागताः ।
धार्तराष्ट्रस्य दुर्बुद्धेर्युद्धे प्रियचिकीर्षवः ॥ २३ ॥

yotsyamänänavekşe ham ya ete'tra samagataḥ

dhartaraṣṭrasya durbuddheyu'ddhe priyacikirṣavah 23.

As we read the stanza, we can almost hear the great warrior's teeth grinding, as he spits out these hot words, which express his mental estimate of his relentless cousins.

Sanjaya said:

24. Thus addressed by Gudakesha, O Bharata, Hrishikesha, having stationed the best of chariots between the two armies;

25. In front of Bhishma and Drona, and all the rulers of the earth, he said, "O Partha, behold these Kurus gathered together".

At a point facing Bhishma, Drona and all the rulers of the earth, the Divine Charioteer pulled up the reins and brought the royal chariot to a halt. As a dutiful driver, Krishna says to Arjuna, "Behold, O Partha! All the Kauravas gathered together". These are the only words that Krishna has spoken in the entire first chapter; and these represent the sparks that set fire to and brought down the egoistic edifice of false valuations, which the great hero had built for himself as a splendid dwelling place for his personality. Hereafter, we shall find how Arjuna reacted to this great challenge and ultimately got his entire 'within' wrecked and shattered.

संजय उवाच

एवमुक्तो हृषीकेशो गुडाकेशेन भारत ।

सेनयोरुभयोर्मध्ये स्थापयित्वा रथोत्तमम् ॥ २४ ॥

Sanjaya uvācha
evamukto hrṣikeso gudakesena
senayorubhayormadhye sthäpayitva rathottamam 24.

भीष्मद्रोणप्रमुखतः सर्वेषां च महीक्षिताम् ।

उवाच पार्थ पश्यैतान्समवेतान्कुरूनिति ॥ २५ ॥

bhismadronapramukhataḥ sarveşăm ca mahikṣitām
uvah partha pasyaitaänsamavetänkuruniti 25.

Partha means 'Son of Pritha'—it is a name of Arjuna; 'Pritha' was another name of Kunti, the Sanskrit term Partha also carries a flavour of the term Parthiva meaning 'clay-made' -'earth-formed'.

The suggestive implication of this term is very striking inasmuch as it connotes that the Gita is the Song-of-Truth sung by the Immortal to the mortal Arjuna, man's all-time representative.

26. Then Partha saw stationed there in both the armies, fathers, grandfathers, teachers, maternal uncles, brothers, sons, grandsons and friends too.

27. (He saw) Fathers-in-law and friends also in both the armies. Then the son of Kunti, seeing all these kinsmen thus standing arrayed, gal spoke thus sorrowfully, filled with deep pity.

तत्रापश्यत्स्थितान्पार्थः पितृनथ पितामहान् ।
आचार्यान्मातुलान्भ्रातृन्पुत्रान्पौत्रान्सखीस्तथा ॥ २६ ॥

tatrapasyatthitänpärtha pitinatha pitamahan
acăyarnmatulanbhratṛnputränpauträsakhimstatha 26."

श्वशुरान्सुहृदवश्चैव सेनयोरुभयोरपि ।
तान्समीक्ष्य स कौन्तेयः सर्वान्बन्धूनवस्थितान् ॥ २७ ॥

Svasuransuhrdascaiva senayorubhyorapi
tansamtkşya sa kaunteyaḥ savarnbandhanavasthitan 27.

Thus shown by Shri Krishna, Arjuna recognised in his enemy lines, all his kith and kin, near and dear family members, brothers and cousins, teachers and grandsires, and almost all his acquaintances and friends. He recognized such intimate relations not only in the enemy lines, but even in his own army. This sight perhaps, brought to his mind, for the first time, the full realisation of the tragedies of a fratricidal war. As a warrior and a man of action, he did not, perhaps until then, fully realize the extent of sacrifice that society would be called upon to make in order that his ambition might be fulfilled and Duryodhana's cruelties avenged.

Whatever might have been the cause, the sight brought into his mind a flood of pity and compassion.

Evidently, this was not an honest emotion. Had it been honest, had his pity and compassion been Buddha-like, natural and instinctive, he would have, even long before the war, behaved quite differently. This emotion which now Sanjaya glorifies as 'pity' in Arjuna, is a misnomer. In the human heart, there is always a great tendency to glorify one's own weaknesses with some convenient angelic name and divine pose. Thus, a rich man's vanity is misnamed as charity when he builds a temple in his own name with the secret aim of immortalising himself. Here also we find that the feeling of desperation that came in Arjuna's mind due to the complete shattering of his mental equilibrium has been misnamed and glorified as 'pity'.

Arjuna had a long life of mental repressions, which had created an infinite amount of dynamic energies seeking a field for expression. His mind got split up because of his egoistic evaluation of himself as the greatest hero of his time, and because of his anxious desire for a victorious end of the war. The preoccupation of his mind, dreaming intensively, about the ultimate end of the war brought about a complete divorce between the subjective and the objective aspects of his mind.

Later on, in this chapter, we shall discover the various symptoms of this neurotic condition in him and his hysterical blabbering which are typical of such a mental patient. The endeavour in Chapter I of the Gita is to give the complete 'case-history of a patient suffering from the typical Arjuna disease', The Bhagwat Gita gives, as I said earlier, an extremely efficient 'Krishna-cure' for this soul-killing 'Arjuna-disease'.

Arjuna said:

28. Seeing these my kinsmen, O Krishna, arrayed, eager to fight,

29. My limbs fail and my mouth is parched, my body quivers and my hair stand on end.

कृपया परयाविष्टो विषीदन्निदमब्रवीत् ।

krpaya parayavisto viṣīdannidamabravit

अर्जुन उवाच—

दृष्ट्वेमं स्वजनं कृष्ण युयुत्सुं समुपस्थितम् ॥ २८ ॥

Arjuna uvacha
drstvemam svajanam krsna yuyutsuch samupasthitam 28.

सीदन्ति मम गात्राणि मुखं च परिशुष्यति ।
वेपथुश्च शरीरे मे रोमहर्षश्च जायते ॥ २९ ॥

sidanti mama gatrani mukham ca pariśusyatim
vepathusca sarire me romaharsasca jayate 29.

In these two stanzas, there is an exhaustive enumeration of the symptoms that the patient could then recognise in his own physical body as a result of his mental confusions. That which Sanjaya had glorified as 'pity', when coming out of Arjuna's own mouth, gains a more realistic expression. Arjuna says "seeing my kinsmen gathered here anxiously determined to fight, my limbs shiver," etc..

All these symptoms are described in the textbooks of modern psychology as typical symptoms of the mental disease named 'anxiety-neurosis'.

30. The Gandiva-bow slips from my hand and my skin burns all ses over; I am also unable to stand and my mind is whirling round, as it were

Here Arjuna is adding some more details of the symptoms of his disease. Earlier we had a list of symptoms that manifested on the physical body. Now in this stanza, Arjuna tries to report recognised-symptoms of the maladjustments at his mental level.

Not only is his mind unsteady, agitated and chaotic, but it has lost all its morale. It has come down to the stupid level of accepting and recognising superstitious omens portending disastrous failures and imminent consequences.

Not only does the following stanza vividly picture to us his mental confusions, but it also shows how far his discrimination has been drained off, and his morale destroyed,

गाण्डीवं स्रंन्सते हस्तात्त्वक्चैव परिदह्यते ।
न च शक्नोम्यवस्थातुं भ्रमतीव च मे मनः ॥ ३० ॥

gandivam sramsate hastattvakcaiva paridahyate
in na ca saknomyavasthätum bhramativa ca me manah 30

31. And I see adverse omens, O Keshava. Nor do I see any good in killing my kinsmen in battle.

In this state of mental confusion, when his emotions have been totally divorced from his intellect, the 'objective-mind', without the guidance of its 'subjective-aspect', runs wild and comes to some unintelligent conclusions. He says, "I desire neither victory, nor empire, nor even pleasure". It is a recognised fact that a patient of hysteria, when allowed to talk, will, in a negative way, express the very cause for the attack. For example, when a woman, hysterically raving, repeatedly declares with all emphasis, that she is not tired of her husband that she still respects him, that he still loves her, that there is no rupture between them, etc., she, by these very words, clearly indicates the exact cause of her mental chaos.

Similarly, the very denials of Arjuna clearly indicate to all careful readers how and why he got into such a state of mental grief. He desired victory. He urgently wanted the kingdom. He anxiously expected to win pleasures for himself and his relations. But the challenging look of the mighty Kaurava forces and the great and eminent warriors standing ready to fight, shattered his hopes, blasted his ambitions, and undermined his self-confidence and he slowly developed the well-known Arjuna-disease, the cure for which is the theme of the Gita.

निमित्तानि च पश्यामि विपरीतानि केशव ।
न च श्रेयोऽनुपश्यामि हत्वा स्वजनमाहवे ॥ ३१ ॥

nimittani ca pasyami viparitani kesava
na ca sreyo nupasyami hatva svajanamáhave 31.

32. For, I desire not victory, O Krishna, nor kingdom, nor pleasures of what avail is dominion to us, O Govinda? Of what avail are pleasures or even life itself?

33. They for whose sake we desire kingdom, enjoyment and pleasures constand here in battle, having renounced life and wealth.

34. Teachers, fathers, sons and also grandfathers, maternal uncles, In thi fathers-in-law, grandsons, brothers-in-law and other relatives.

Arjuna continues his arguments to Krishna against the advisability of such a civil war between the two factions of the same royal family. A Dharma-hunting Arjuna is here mentally manufacturing a case for himself justifying his cowardly retreat from the post of duty where destiny has called upon him to act.

न काङ्क्षे विजय कृष्ण न च राज्यं सुखानि च ।
किं नो राज्येन गोविन्द किं भोगैर्जीवितेन वा ॥ ३२ ॥

na kanksṣe vijayam krsna na ca räpyam sukhani ca
kim no rajyena govinda kim bhogaurjivitena va 32.

येषामर्थे काङ्क्षितं नो राज्यं भोगाः सुखानि च।
त इमेऽवस्थिता युद्धे प्राणांस्त्यक्त्वा धनानि च ॥ ३३ ॥

yeşamarthe kanikṣatam no rajyam sukhani ca
ta ime vasthita yuddhe pranamstkva dhanani ca 33.

आचार्याः पितरः पुत्रास्तथैव च पितामहाः ।
मातुलाः श्वशुराः पौत्राः श्यालाः सम्बन्धिनस्तथा ॥ ३४ ॥

acayarḥ pitaraḥ putrastathaiva ca pitamahah
matulaḥ śvasuraḥ pautrah syalah sambandhinastatha 34.

He repeats what he had said earlier because Krishna, with his pregnant silence, is criticizing Arjuna's attitude. The provocatively smiling lips of the Lord are whipping Arjuna into a sense of shame. He wants the moral support of his friend and charioteer to come to the conclusion that what he is feeling in his own mind is acceptable and just. But the endorsement and the intellectual sanction are not forthcoming from either the look of Krishna or the Lord's words..

35. These I do not wish to kill, though they may kill me. O Madhusudana, even for the sake of dominion over the three worlds; how much less for the sake of the earth.

Feeling that he had not expressed his case strongly enough to Krishna, to make him come to this conclusion, and, assuming that it was because of this that the Lord had not given his assent to it, Arjuna therefore, decided to declare with a mock spirit of renunciation, that he had so much large-heartedness in him that he would not kill his cousins, even if they were to kill him. The climax came when Arjuna, with quixotic exaggeration, declared that he would not fight the war, even if he were to win all the three worlds of the universe, much less so, for the mere Hastinapura-kingship.

एतान्न हन्तुमिच्छामि घ्नतोऽपि मधुसूदन ।
अपि त्रैलोक्यराज्यस्य हेतोः किं नु महीकृते ॥ ३५ ॥

etanna hantumicchami ghnato'pi madhustidana
api trailokyarajyasya hetoḥ kim nu mahikṛte 35.

36. Killing these sons of Dhritarashtra, what pleasure can be ours, O Janardana? Sin alone will be our gain by killing these felons.

In spite of all that Arjuna said so far, Krishna is as silent as a sphinx. Therefore, Arjuna gives up his melodramatic expression and assumes a softer, a more appealing tone and takes the attitude of explaining in vain, a serious matter to a dull-witted friend. The change of strategy becomes conspicuously ludicrous when we notice Krishna's continued silence!!

In the first line of the stanza he explains to Krishna that no good can arise out of killing the sons of Dhritarashtra. Still, the wooden-smile of Krishna does not change and the Pandava hero, his intelligence shattered, tries to find a cause for Krishna's attitude. Immediately, he remembers that the Kaurava brothers were behaving towards the Pandavas as felons. Atatayinah means felons, who deserve to be killed according to the Artha Shastra.

निहत्य धार्तराष्ट्रान्नः का प्रीतिः स्याज्जनार्दन।
पापमेवाश्रयेदस्मान्हत्वैतानाततायिनः ॥ ३६ ॥

nihatya dhartaraṣṭrannaḥ ka pritiḥ syajjanardana
papamevasrayedasmän hatvaitanatatayinah 36.

"Whether he be a preceptor, an old man, or a Veda-knowing Brahmana, if he comes in front as an Atatai (felon) he should be killed on the spot without a thought. There is no sin involved in killing a felon." (Manu.VIII- 350-351)

Sin is only a mistake committed by a misunderstood individual ego against its own Divine Nature as the Eternal Soul. To act as the body, the mind, or the intellect is not to act up to the responsibilities of a man but it becomes an attempt to behave under the impulses of an animal. All those acts performed and motives entertained, which create grosser mental impressions and thereby, build stronger walls between us and our cognition of the Real Divine Spark in ourselves, are called sins.

Arjuna's seemingly learned objection to killing enemies is a misinterpretation of our sacred texts (shastra), and to have acted upon it would have been suicidal to our very culture, Therefore, Krishna refuses to show any sign either of appreciation or criticism of Arjuna's stand. The Lord understands that his friend is raving hysterically and the best policy is to allow a mental patient first of all to bring out everything in his mind and thus exhaust himself.

37. Therefore, we shall not kill the sons of Dhritarashtra, our relatives; for how can we be happy by killing our own people, O Madhava?

Here, Arjuna concludes his seemingly logical arguments u scriptu which have got a false look of Hindu scriptural sanction. More than deliberate blasphemers of a scripture, the unconscious misinterpreters of a sacred text are the innocent criminals who bring about the wretched downfall of its philosophy. Purring with the satisfaction of a cat in the kitchen, Arjuna, in this verse, is rounding up his arguments and coming to the dangerous conclusion that he should not kill the aggressors, nor face their heartless challenge! Even then, Krishna is silent.

तस्मान्नार्हा वयं हन्तुं धार्तराष्ट्रान्स्वबान्धवान्।
स्वजनं हि कथं हत्वा सुखिनः स्याम माधव ॥ ३७ ॥

tasmannahar tayar hantun dhortandstränsvabandhavan
svajanam hi katham hatva sukhinah syama madhava 37.

Arjun's discomfiture makes him really quite conspicuous in his ugliness. In the second line of the stanza, he makes a personal appeal to Krishna and almost begs of him to think for himself and endorse Partha's own lunatic conclusions.

With the familiarity born out of his long-standing friendship, Arjuna addresses his charioteer with affection as Madhava, and asks him how one can come to any happiness after one has destroyed one's own kinsmen. Still, Krishna remains silent.

38. Though these, with their intelligence clouded by greed, see no evil in the destruction of the families in the society, and no q eid bassin in their cruelty to friends...

39. Why should not we, who clearly see evil in the destruction of the family-units, learn to turn away from this sin, O Janardana?

यद्यप्येते न पश्यन्ति लोभोपहतचेतसः ।
कुलक्षयकृतं दोषं मित्रद्रोहे च पातकम् ॥ ३८ ॥

yadyapyete na pasyanti lobhopahatacetasah
kulakṣayakṛtam dosamh mitradrohe ca patakam 38.

कथं न ज्ञेयमस्माभिः पापादस्मान्निवर्तितुम् ।
कुलक्षयकृतं दोषं प्रपश्यद्भिर्जनार्दन ॥ ३९ ॥

katham na jñeyamasmabhiḥ papadasmännivartitum
kulakṣayakytam dosam prapasyadibharjanardana 39.

No doubt, the Kauravas, grown blind in their greed for power and wealth, cannot see the destruction of the entire social structure by this war. Their ambition has so completely clouded their intelligence and sensibility that they fail to appreciate or understand the cruelty in annihilating their own friends.

But Arjuna seems to retain his reasoning capacity and can clearly foresee the chaos in which society will get buried by this fratricidal war. Now his argument amounts to this, if a friend of ours, in his drunkenness, behaves nastily, it would be worse than drunkenness in us, if we were to retaliate; for, we are expected to know that our friend, with his fumed-up intelligence, does not entertain enough discriminative awareness of what he is doing. At such moments, it would be our duty to forgive the mischief and overlook the impudence.

Similarly, here, Arjuna argues: "If Duryodhana and his friends are behaving as blind aggressors, should the Pandavas not retire quietly and suffer the ignominy of a defeat, and consider it their dutiful offering at the altar of peace?" How far this philosophy is dangerous in itself will be seen as we read more and more the passages of the Gita and come to appreciate the pith of its philosophy which is the very kernel of our Hindu way-of-living. "Active resistance to evil" is the central idea in the doctrine expounded by Krishna in the Gita.

40. In the destruction of a family, the immemorial religious rites of that family perish, on the destruction of spirituality, impiety overcomes the whole family.

Just as a storyteller comes to add new details each time he narrates the same old story, so too, Arjuna seems to draw new inspiration from his foolishness, and each time his creative intelligence puts forth fresh arguments in support of his wrong philosophy. As soon as he finishes a stanza, he gets, as it were, a new lease of arguments to prattle, and takes refuge behind their noise.

He indicates here that, when individual families are destroyed, along with them the religious traditions of the society will also end, and soon an era of impiety will be ushered in.

Cultural experiments were the preoccupations of our fore fathers and they knew that the culture and tradition of each family was a unit of the total culture and integrity of the whole nation. Hence the importance of the family-Dharma so seriously brought forth by Arjuna as an argument against this civil war.

कुलक्षये प्रणश्यन्ति कुलधर्माः सनातनाः ।
धर्मे नष्टे कुलं कृत्स्नमधर्मोऽभिभवत्युत ॥ ४० ॥

kulakṣaye pransyanti kuladhamarh sanatanah
dharme naşte kulam krisvamadharmoa bhibhavatyuta 40

41. By the prevalence of impiety, O Krishna, the women of the family become corrupt and women being corrupted, O descendent of the Vrishni-clan, there arises intermingling of castes (Varuna-Samkara).

Continuing the argument of the previous verse, Partha declares the consequences that will follow when the true moral integrity of the families is destroyed. Slowly the morality in the society will wane and there will be an 'admixture of castes'.

Caste is a word, which, in its perverted meaning, has recently come in for a lot of criticism from the educated; and they, no doubt, are all justified, if caste, in reality means what we understand it to be in our society today. But what we witness around us, in the name of caste, is the ugly decadence into which the Hindu way-of-living has fallen. Caste, in those days, was conceived of as an intelligent division of the available manpower in the community on the basis of intellectual and mental capacities of the individuals.

Those who were intellectuals and had a passion for research and study were styled Brahmanas (Brahmins); those who had political ambitions for leadership and took upon themselves the risky art of maintaining peace and plenty and saving the country from internal and external aggressions, were called the Kshatriyas; those who served the community through agriculture and trade were the Vaishyas and, lastly, all those who did not fall in any of the above categories were styled as Shudras, whose duties in society were service and labour. Our modern social workers and officials, agricultural and industrial labourers all must fall under this noble category!

अधर्माभिभवात्कृष्ण प्रदुष्यन्ति कुलस्त्रिय।
स्त्रीषु दृष्टासु वार्ष्णेय जायते वर्णङ्करः ॥ ४१ ॥

adhamarbhibhakrsna pradasanti kulastriyah
strişu dustasu vārsneya jayate varnasankara 41.

In the largest scope of its implication, when we thus understand the caste-system, it is the same as today's professional groups. Therefore, when they talk so seriously about the inadvisability of 'admixture of the castes', they only mean what we already know to be true in our own social pattern. An engineer in charge of a hospital and working in the operation-theatre as a doctor would be a social danger, as much as a doctor would be if he is appointed as an officer for planning, guiding and executing a hydroelectric scheme!

When the general morality of society has decayed; the young men and women, blinded by uncontrolled passion, start mingling without restraint. And lust knows no logic and cares least for better evolution or better culture. There will be thereafter, unhealthy intermingling of incompatible cultural traits.

42. 'Confusion of castes' leads the slayer of the family to hell; for 996 of put their forefathers fall, deprived of the offerings of PINDA (rice-ball) and water (libations).

सङ्करो नरकायैव कुलघ्नानां कुलस्य च ।
पतन्ति पितरो ह्येषां लुप्तपिण्डोदकक्रियाः ॥ ४२ ॥

sankro narakayaiva kulaghnanam kulasya ca
patanti pitaro hyesan luptapindodakakriyah 42

The argument is still continued and Arjuna points out the consequences of caste-admixture. When confusion of the castes has taken place, both, outside in the moral life of true discipline and in one's own inner temperament, then the family tradition gets flouted and ruined.

In the context of our discourses, we must understand that to the dead, it is bread-and-water; to see that their survivors maintain and continue the cultural purity that they themselves had so laboriously cultivated and inculcated into the minds of their children. In case the society squanders away its culture, so laboriously built up as a result of the slow blossoming of the social values of life through generations of careful cultivation, we will be insulting the very labours of our ancestors. It is attractive and poetic, indeed, to conceive of the dead as watching over their survivors and observing their ways of living from the balcony of their heavenly abode! It would certainly be as painful as the pains of hunger and thirst to them if they were to find that their survivors were deliberately making a jungle of their laboriously laid gardens. Understood thus, the entire stanza appears to be very appropriate.

Each generation passes down the torch of its culture to the next generation, its children, and it is for them to preserve, tend and nourish that torch and hand it over carefully to the succeeding generation, if not more, at least no less bright, than when they got it.

In India, the sages discovered and initiated a culture that is spiritual, and this spiritual culture is maintained and worked out through religious practices, and therefore, culture and religion are, to the Hindu, one and the same. Very rarely we find any mention of the term culture, as such, in our ancient literature. More often we meet with the insistence on and the mention of our religious practices.

In fact, the Hindu religion is a technique by which this spiritual culture can be maintained and worked out in the community. Therefore, we find in these stanzas, and in similar contexts, always an enthusiastic emphasis upon the religious life, whether it be in the family or in the society. Dharma comprises those divine values of life by living which we manifest more and more the essential spiritual being in us. Family-Dharma (Kuladharma) is thus nothing but the rules of living, thinking, and acting in a united, well-planned family. By strictly following these rules we soon come to learn in the prayer-rooms of our homes, how to live as better citizens of the Aryan-culture.

43. By these evil deeds of the 'destroyers of the family', which cause confusion of castes, the eternal religious rites of the ta bla caste and the family are destroyed.

What was said in the discourse upon the last stanza will become amply clear by this statement of Arjuna. Here also he bemoans that as a result of the civil war, the religious traditions of the family will all be lost and when he says so, as I have said earlier, if we understand religion as the spiritual culture of India, the training for which was primarily given in the individual homes, then the stanza becomes self-explanatory. We also know that after a war there is a sudden cracking up of the existing cultural values in any society. Our modern world which is panting and sighing under the burden of its own immoralities and deceits, is an example of how war brings about not only disabled men with amputated limbs, but also deeper ulcers and uglier deformities in their mental make-up,

दोषैरेतैः कुलघ्नानां वर्णसङ्करकारकैः ।
उत्साद्यन्ते जातिधर्माः कुलधर्माश्च शाश्वताः ॥ ४३ ॥

dosairetaiḥ kulaghnanam varnasankarakarakaih
utsadyante jätidhamarh kuladhamarsca sasvatah 43

In these words, we can detect in Arjuna almost the world's first conscientious objector to war! In these passages he offers a splendid series of pacifist arguments good for all times!!

44. We have heard, O Janardana, that it is inevitable for those men, in whose families the religious practices have been destroyed, to dwell in hell for an unknown period of time.

Krishna still refuses to speak. Arjuna has come to a point where he can neither stop talking nor find any more arguments. Strangely compelling is the grace of the Lord's dignified silence. Here in this stanza, Arjuna almost concludes his arguments and mentions the tradition which he had heard that "men whose family-religion has broken down will go to hell"

But, on the other hand, when we understand the statement in all its scientific implications, even the worst of us will feel the immediate urgency for revolutionising our point of view. We have already seen that the family-Dharma means only the cultural purity in the family, which is the unit of the community. We also found that since their culture is essentially spiritual, to the Hindus 'religion is culture.

उत्सन्नकुलधर्माणां मनुष्याणां जनार्दन।
नरकेऽनियतं वासो भवतीत्यनुशुश्रुम ॥ ४४ ॥

utsannkuladhamārṇām manuṣyānam janardana
narake'niyatam vaso bhavatityanusuśruma 44.

So, Arjuna implies that when the unity of home-life is shattered, and when purity of living and sanctity of thought are destroyed in the individual home-life, the generation that has caused such a shattering is ordering for itself and for others, a melancholy era of hellish sorrows and sufferings.

45. Alas! We are involved in a great sin, in that we are prepared to kill our kinsmen, from greed for the pleasures of the kingdom.

Though pitiable, it is indeed pleasantly ludicrous to watch Arjuna's intellectual exhaustion and emotional weariness as expressed in this verse. In his effeminate lack of self-confidence he bemoans here, "Alas! We are involved" etc. These words clearly show that instead of becoming a master of the situation, Arjuna is now a victim of it. He has not the virile confidence that he is the master of the circumstances and therefore, with a creeping sense of growing inner cowardice, he feels almost helplessly persecuted.

This unhealthy mental weakness drains off his heroism and he desperately tries to put a paper-crown upon his cowardice, to make it look divine and angelic, and to parade it as 'pity'. Thus, he of the war and imputes a low motive to the righteous war simply because he wants to justify his pacifist idea, which does not instinctively gurgle out from his known strength, but which oozes out from his ulcerated mind.

अहो बत महत्पापं कर्तुं व्यवसिता वयम्।
यद्राज्यसुखलोभेन हन्तुं स्वजनमुद्यताः ॥ ४५ ॥

aho bata mahatpapam kartum vyavasita vayam
yadrajyasukhalobbena hantum sejanamudyath 45

46. If the sons of Dhritarashtra weapons-in-hand, slay me in battle, unresisting and unarmed, that would be better for me.

Here, Arjuna declares his FINAL opinion that, under the 2nd circumstances narrated during his long-drawn limping arguments, it is better for him to die in battle unresisting and unarmed, even if the Kauravas were to shoot him down, like a hunted deer, with a dozen arrows piercing his royal body!

The word that Arjuna uses here is particularly to be noted. The texture of the word used is, in itself, a great commentary upon the thought in the mind of the one who has made the statement... Kshema is the material and physical victory, while Moksha is the spiritual Self-mastery: Though Arjuna's arguments were all labouring hard to paint the idea, that to have fought that war was against the spiritual culture of the country (Moksha), he himself stated in his conclusions that not to fight this war would be a material blessing (Kshema) inasmuch as an escape from the battlefield now is to gain, perhaps, sure physical security !!

यदि मामप्रतीकारमशस्त्रं शस्त्रपाणयः।
धार्तराष्ट्रा रणे हन्युस्तन्मे क्षेमतरं भवेत् ॥ ४६ ॥

yadi mamapratikaramalastram sastrapanayah
dhartarastra rane hanyustanme kṣemataram bhavet 46.

In short, anxiety for the fruit-of-his-action (victory in battle) demoralised Arjuna and he got himself into an anxiety state-neurosis,

Sanjaya said:

47. Having thus spoken in the midst of the battlefield, Arjuna sat down on the seat of the chariot, casting away his bow and arrows, with a mind distressed with sorrow.

The concluding stanza of this chapter contains the words of Sanjaya in which he gave the running commentary of what he saw on the battlefield. Exhausted by his weary arguments, Arjuna, completely shattered within, sank back on the flag-staff in the open chariot, throwing down his kingly weapons.

This is the scene at which we shall leave Arjuna in the First Chapter of the Gita.

Thus, in the Upanishads of the glorious Bhagwat Gita, in the Science of the Eternal, in the scripture of Yoga, in the dialogue between Sri Krishna and Arjuna, the first discourse ends entitled:

The Yoga of the Arjuna-Grief

In the scriptural textbooks of ancient times, the end of a chapter was indicated by some sign or symbol. In modern days, this is not necessary, in much we have the passages in print before us and we can see that one section or chapter has ended and another has begun. Even here, the printers have to mark the end of one chapter and, by a separate title, indicate the beginning of the next.

संजय उवाच—

एवमुक्त्वार्जुनः संख्ये रथोपस्थ उपाविशत् ।

विसृज्य सशरं चापं शोकसंविग्नमानसः ॥ ४७ ॥

Sanjaya uvacha
evamuktvarjunah sankhye rathopasttha upavisat
visrjya sasaram capa sokasmvingnamanasah 47.

In olden days, it was much more difficult, since books were not printed, and each student got during his study a new edition of the scripture printed on the memory-slabs of his own mind. Since scripture-study was in those days from mouth to mouth, the students had to memorise whole textbooks and chant them daily. In such a case, it was necessary to have some word or words to inform both the reciter and the listeners as to the ending of a section and the fresh beginning of another. This was done by some conventional symbols.

In the Upanishads, the accepted method was to recite the last Mantra or the concluding portion of the last Mantra of the chapter twice. In the Gita, however, we have the repetition of a statement, which may be considered as an epilogue, in Sanskrit called a Sankalpa Vakya. The same Sankalpa is repeated at the end of each chapter, the difference being only that at the end of each chapter, the chapter-number is mentioned, along with the special title of that chapter.

The Gita Sankalpa Vakya (Epilogue) is a beautiful statement of pregnant words conveying a wealth of details regarding the very textbook. Shrimad Bhagwat Gita has been considered here as an Upanishad nay, each chapter in the Gita is considered as an Upanishad, and among the eighteen Upanishads, together constituting the Divine Song, we here end the first of them, entitled THE YOGA OF ARJUNA'S DESPONDENCY. These chapters are called Upanishads because they are declarations concealing such deep significance that a hasty reader will miss their full import, unless he does long and intense meditation over the wealth of suggestive meaning that lies concealed behind the simple-looking stanzas. As in the Upanishads, here also we need the help of a sympathetic teacher who can train us in the art of opening the seven hundred lockers in the treasure chamber of the Gita.

Upanishad is a word indicating a literature that is to be studied by sitting (shad), near (upa) a teacher, in a spirit of receptive meekness and surrender (ni). The contents of the scriptural textbooks are all over the world always the same. They teach us that there is a changeless Reality behind the ever-changing phenomenal world of perceptions, feelings and understanding. This great Advaitic Truth as declared in the Hindu scriptural textbooks is termed the Brahman and, therefore, the textbook that teaches us the nature of Brahman and shows us the means of realising it is called Brahman-knowledge (Brahma-Vidya).

Unlike western philosophy, among the Aryans, a theory is accepted as a philosophy only when the philosopher prescribes for us a practical technique by which all seekers can come to discover and experience for themselves the goal indicated in that philosophy. Thus, in all Hindu philosophies there are two distinct sections: one explains the theory and the other describing the technique of practice. The portion that explains the technique of living the philosophy and coming to a close subjective experience is called Yoga Shastra.

The word Yoga comes from the root Yuj, that means to join. Any conscious attempt on the part of an individual to lift his present available personality and attune it to a higher, perfect ideal is called Yoga and the science of Yoga is called Yoga Shastra. Since in this epilogue, the Gita is called a Yoga Shastra, we must expect to discover in the Song of the Lord not only airy philosophical expositions of a Truth-too subtle for the ordinary man to grasp, but also instructions by which, every one of us can hope to reach, step by step, the giddy heights of the Divine pinnacles, that stand eternally swathed in the transcendental glory of Absolute Perfection.

The theme of philosophy and Yoga cannot be very attractive to the ordinary men of the world because it is so scientific and it deals with imperceptible ideologies. Mathematics cannot be thrilling reading except for a mathematician; and mathematics can very well afford to ignore those who have no taste for it. But religion tries to serve all and the anxiety of all prophets is to serve every one in all generations. Thus, in order to tame a difficult theme and to contain it within the ambit of a textbook of universal acceptance, the teachers of olden times had to discover methods by which the subjective ideologies could be given an appealing look of substantial objectivity. This was done by giving a detailed picture of the teacher, so that in our mental image he is so much familiarised, that we feel his words also as something very familiar to us.

In the tradition of the Hindu textbooks, the great Rishis worked out the subtle ideas containing the crystallised truths into an easily digestible capsule called Dharma. In the Upanishads, we have a complete picture of a teacher and a taught painted with hasty strokes, unfinished, and rough. In the Geet a on the other hand, it being a philosophical discourse embedded in the mythology of the nation, we find a finished picture, palpitating with life, against a scintillating situation, wherein the very same ancient truths have been reasserted.

Lord Krishna is now made to repeat the Upanishadic Truths in the context of a great conflict, to serve his life-long friend Arjuna, who is shown as seriously suffering from a total mental rupture. Therefore, we shall expect in the Gita a much more sympathetic explanation and guidance than when the same truths came out from the inspired saints, who were not as much in contact with the weaknesses of ordinary mortals. This glory of the Gita has been indicated here when the Sankalpa Vakya says that it is a conversation between the Lord and a mortal.

This chapter is called by a self-contradicting title. It is named as the "Yoga of Arjuna's Grief". If 'grief' could be Yoga, almost all of us, without a choice, are already Yogins. In the commentary of this chapter, I indicated that the Arjuna-condition of utter despair is the auspicious mental attitude wherein the Gita-seeds are to be sown, and the flowers of Krishna-perfection gathered. Be it in an individual or a society, in a community or a nation, religion and philosophy will be in demand only when the heart has come to experience the Arjuna-grief.

To the extent that the world of today has felt its incompetence to face the battle of life, not daring to destroy their near and dear values of economic expansion and industrial lust, to that extent it is fit for listening to the message of the Gita. Just as the act of cooking, by itself, is not fulfilled without the eating that follows, so also, in spite of the best that may be available in life, a sense of incompleteness is felt and a deep hunger to gain a better awareness and a fuller existence in the world is experienced The scriptural texts cannot, in themselves, help any one. Since this mental condition is so unavoidable before the actual Yoga is started, even the initial mental condition is called by a wishful anticipation, as Yoga. For learning and living the Gita, the Arjuna-condition is the initial sadhana.

Om Om Om Om Om

ॐ तत्सदिति श्रीमद् भगवद् गीतासूपनिषत्सु ब्रह्मविद्यायां
योगशास्त्रे श्रीकृष्णार्जुनसम्वादे अर्जुनविषादयोगो नाम प्रथमोऽध्यायः

Om tatsaditi srimadbhagavadgitasi apanisatsu brahmavidyāyāṁ yogasastre śri krsnarjuna samvade arjunaviṣadayogo nama prathamo'dhyayah

Excerpts from the The Gita by Swami Chinmayananda Saraswati.

❑

Chapter-1

Supreme Peace (Param Shanti)—The Goal of Life is labelled here as the great peace that knows no diminution. In these days of peace-mongers getting ready for war in the name of peace, one is apt to become honestly skeptical about the goal indicated in this stanza. The term 'peace' here is not that undefined vague concept that is often repeated in politics, whenever it is convenient for a set of politicians to do so, but the term 'shanti' has a wealth of psychological suggestiveness.

It is very well known that every living creature is, at all moments, trying to gain a better happiness, through all its activities in life. From breathing and eating, to the organised endeavour in capturing the world-market through war and destruction, all activities are attempts by the frail individuals to discover a greater and a better joy or happiness. This is true not only in man but in the animal kingdom, and even in the vegetable world. In short, no action is possible unless the actor is motivated by an inner urge in him to seek a greater sense of fulfilment or joy unto himself.

If thus, the whole world is striving to win the highest joy that it possibly can, and having gained it, to invest all energy and intelligence to retain the same, then the goal of life should be Absolute Happiness, where all strife ends, all desires are fulfilled, all thoughts and agitations are finally exhausted. Desires for joy give rise to thought disturbances, which, trying to fulfil themselves in the outer world, become the visible actions in everyday life.

The restlessness of the mind and the weary fatigue of the body shall both end, when Joy is attained. Therefore, Absolute Joy is Absolute Peace.

Here, in this stanza the Goal of Life is indicated as the Supreme Peace, which may be, in other words, explained as the Supreme Joy.

"Thou Shalt Not Doubt This, for Doubt is most Sinful." How?... Listen:

40. The ignorant, the faithless, the doubting-self goes to destruction; there is neither this world, nor the other, nor happiness for the doubter.

In the previous verse, it was said that those who had faith and knowledge would soon reach the Supreme Peace. In order to hammer this very same Truth in, Krishna is here emphasising through a negative declaration that they, who have NOT these qualities cultivated, gained and developed in them, will get themselves ultimately destroyed and completely ruined. He who has neither the Knowledge of the Self-if not a spiritual realisation, at least a clear intellectual understanding—nor 'the intellectual readiness to grapple with and fully understand the true import of the scriptural declarations and the words of the Masters' (shraddha), Krishna asserts, will certainly get ruined, if he be also a 'doubting Thomas' (samshaya-atma).

In the next line, Krishna, with all emphasis, condemns such men of endless doubts, and points out their tragedy in life. The Lord says that such men who Doubt the Self will not find any joy or happiness anywhere neither here nor in the hereafter. In explaining thus, the Greta seems to express that there may be a small chance perhaps, for one who is devoid of knowledge and faith to discover some kind of a happiness in this world, here and now, but that those who are constant doubters can enjoy neither here nor there. Such men are psychologically incapable of enjoying any situation, because the doubting tendency in them will poison all their experiences. He whose teeth have become septic, must constantly poison the food that he is taking; so too, those who have this tendency of doubting everything, will never be able to accommodate themselves to any situation, however perfect and just it might be. The line contains a spot of satire, almost vitriolic in its pungency, when it is directed against the intelligent skeptic.

अज्ञश्चाश्रद्दधानश्च संशयात्मा विनश्यति ।
नायं लोकोऽस्ति न परो न सुखं संशयात्मनः ॥ ४० ॥

ajascaddaddhanaśca samsayatma vinasyati
nayam loko'sti na paro na sukham samsayatmanah 40.

WHEREFORE FOR THIS REASON ONLY:

41. He who has renounced actions by YOGA, whose doubts are o rent as under by 'Knowledge', who is self-possessed, actions do not bind him, O Dhananjaya

This being the penultimate verse in the chapter, is a beautiful summary of all the main secrets of life explained at length in it. When, through the practice of Karma Yoga, we have learnt to renounce our attachments to the fruits of action, and yet to work on in perfect detachment when doubt in us regarding the Goal of Life has been completely removed in our own inner experiences of the nobler and the diviner in us—as a result of the above two, the ego comes to rediscover itself to be nothing other than the Atman. Then the individual ego comes to live POISED IN THE SELF AS THE SELF. When such an individual works, his actions can never bind him.

योगसंन्यस्तकर्माणं ज्ञानसञ्छित्वसंशयम् ।
आत्मवन्तं न कर्माणि निबध्नन्ति धनञ्जय ॥ ४१ ॥

yogasannyastakarmanam janasañchinnasamsayam
atmavantam na karmani nibandhanti dhananjaya 41.

It is only egoistic activities motivated by our egocentric desires that leave gross impressions on our inner personality, and thus painfully bind us to reap their reactions. With a sense of detachment and in right-knowledge, as indicated in the above scheme, when an individual has destroyed his ego-sense, his actions cannot bind him at all. As a dreamer, I might commit a murder in my dream upon my dream-wife. But when I awake from my dream, I shall not be punished for the crime that I seem to have committed in my dream. For, the dreamer has also ended along with the dream. The dreamer committed the murder and deserves punishment; but in the waker, the dreamer is absent. Similarly, the egocentric actions can bind and throttle only the ego, but when the ego has become Atmavantah, meaning POISED IN THE SELF—just like the dreamer when he gets poised in the waker—the activities of the ego can no more bind the Self. The ego POISED IN THE SELF, is the experience of the Real Self; the dreamer poised in the waker, is the waker.

THIS BEING THE WONDROUS RESULT AND THE SUPREME PROFIT THAT TRUE-KNOWLEDGE CAN GIVE TO THE DELUDED, KRISHNA ADVISES ARJUNA:

42. Het chal Therefore with the sword of Knowledge, cut asunder the doubt of the Self, born of
ignorance, residing in your heart, and take refuge in 'YOGA'. Arise, O Bharata.

In this concluding stanza the Lord's advice is precise and it is given with a loving insistence. The stanza rings with a spirit of paternal urgency felt by the Lord towards the Pandava Prince.

In the language of war, Krishna advises his warrior-friend on the battlefield, how best to live the life of dedication and perfection as advised by the Hindu Rishis from the quiet and peaceful Himalayan valleys. With the sword of Knowledge, Arjuna is encouraged to cut off the bonds of ignorance and cleave asunder this doubt of the self lying in the heart.

The spiritual doubt is explained here as working from the heart. This may read rather strange to a modern man: doubt must come from the intellect; it cannot come from the heart.

It is the traditional belief in Vedanta that 'the intellect is seated in the heart', wherein the term HEART does not mean the fleshy pumping-instrument in the human bosom. The term HEART is used here not in its physiological meaning but in its literacy usage, where HEART means the source of all love and sympathy of all noble human emotions. An intellect functioning from and through an atmosphere of sympathetic love, kindly charity and such other noble qualities alone can be considered in the science of philosophy as the human reason. Therefore, when the Upanishads talk of the doubts lying crystallised in the heart, the Rishis mean the intellectual perversions in some of the seekers that make them incompetent to feel and appreciate the vision of the Soul.

तस्मादज्ञानसंभूतं हृत्स्थं ज्ञानासिनात्मनः ।
छित्त्वैन सञ्जय योगमातिष्ठोतिष्ठ भारत ॥ ४२ ॥

tasmadajñanasambhutam hrestham jaanasinatmanah
chittvainam samayam yogamatistottista bhatrata 42.

These doubts can be completely annihilated only when the individual gains an intimate, subjective experience of the Self in him.

This can be achieved only by Yoga—NOT a strange mystical process, secretly advised to a few, by mysteriously rare groups of Gurus, to be practised in the unknown dark caves of the Himalayas, living altogether a frightful life of unnatural privations. In the Gita, the word Yoga has been forever tamed and domesticated to be with all of us, serving us faithfully at all times in our life. By the term Yoga, in this last stanza, Krishna means the 'twelve techniques' which He has explained as the subjective-Yajnas.

The chapter concludes with a spirited call to Arjuna "Arise, O Bharata". In the context of the Gita, though the word may be rightly said to mean only a call to Arjuna, it is a call to every seeker, especially to this country as a whole, to get up and act well in the spirit of Yajna, and thereby, to gain more and more inner purity, so that through true meditation everyone of us can come to experience and gain the Supreme Peace which is the final fulfilment of evolution.

Thus, in the UPANISHADS of the glorious Bhagwat Gita, in the Science of the Eternal, in the scripture of YOGA, in the dialogue between Sri Krishna and Arjuna, the fourth discourse ends entitled:

The Yoga of Renunciation of Action In Knowledge

Om Om Om Om Om

ॐ तत्सदिति श्रीमद् भगवद् गीतासूपनिषत्सु ब्रह्मविद्यायां
योगशास्त्रे श्रीकृष्णार्जुनसंवादे ज्ञानकर्मसंन्यासयोगो नाम
चतुर्थोऽध्यायः

Om tatsaditi Srimad bhagavad gitasü üpanişatsu
brahmavidyāyām
yogasastre śrī krşņarjuna samvade jäänakarmasannyasayogo
nama chaturtho'dhyayah

Excerpts have been taken from the *The Gita* by Swami Chinmayananda Saraswati. While reading his deliberation on this holy text, I realised a deep and profounding need to come forward infront of the readers with my own understanding of this Holy text.

❑

Chapter-2

Gita is the Song of the Truth—Sung by the immortal to the moral Arjuna man's all time representatives Arjuna is also referred as partha meaning clay made as earth formed. Thus this divine lesson is from Heaven above for lower mortals on how they can lead their lives in a better way.

Even in today's scenario we recognise that in our human heart we have a great tendency to glorify one's own weakness and failures with some convenient angelic and divine pose. Most of the times our shattering of mental equilibrium is glorified in a sense of giving it a name of pity, defeat, anxiety, depression, falives, torture, and whatnot.

Most of the times we fall into this trap of mental weakness for our egocentric personality gets shattered when we suffer failures. We place much importance on our strength and are unable to accept our defeat and our mind splits up.

Shrimad Bhagwat Gita the most sacred book of the Hindu and the revelation of the divine truth from the mouth of the God occurs in the Bhishma parva of the Mahabharata and comprises eighteen chapter from the 25th to 42nd.

This great handbook of practical living market a great spiritual and social revolution in Hinduism and set the stage for the right moral conduct.

In a way Shrimad Bhagwat Gita set the path for the renaissance in the sanatan Dharma and perpetuated the path of right conduct and right action in the ages that followed the puranic Era.

Shrimad Bhagwat Gita is a treatise of the instruction as to the conduct and way of life to be followed by a person and to imitate the subtle philosophical principles of the Vedanta in the day-to-day life of an individual.

Mahabharata and Gita have been texts very close to the just way of life and its slokas offer for a student having reached a threshold in his life wanting to plunge into the life of a Crista the way out of dilemma and confusion.

This is a book which not only offers solace to the distracted and confused mind but also shows us the right path in our life.

This holybook is the song of the lead on the holy revelation from the ultimate truth the Lord Venkatesh Krishna in this stride reveals his true self to the parth—The Arjuna who has lost semblance and is unable to take the right decision.

The holy war on the Dharam yuddh at Kurukshetra is akin to our own lives, at every step we are fighting the war in the outer world and a war is going within ourselves.

This is the first and supposedly the first only book which acknowledges human follies weaknesses and shortcomings and gives solutions and recesses with answers which are often relevant today.

Probably no other text in the world deals with human weaknesses and offers solutions which are relevant even in today's scenario and context.

In the saying of the Lord in the Gita - the poet Rishi Vyasa has brought the vedic truth from the reavestered Himalaya Caves a knowledge which were kept secret by few reverend reeves to the active fields of practical life and warfare.

Arjuna the hero, the most talented one, the one who is all prepared with the expertise and knowledge to face the challenges of life head on gel's perturbed and distributed in the battlefield when the actual challenges comes his way.

This shows that even today we might have all the knowledge, expertise and wisdom to face the challenges of life but if we lack a stable character and a quiet mind all the Gyan' is but put to waste. The real mind of our potential is when we can arise from the challenges of life undisturbed, face life problem with a calm and composed mind and see beyond what would we perceive through our senses a Gyan and then in the true worldly sense we are the unique the cowera of the say. One who has learnt the art to content the mind has learnt the art to win our life. He is thus a Vijeta—an undisputed master in the game of life.

When the battle of life begins then many a times because of stress and psychological maladjustment we are not able to face life with full savage and strength.

Shrimad Bhagwat Gita a treatise on human psychology relates the correct action during trauma and distress.

Arjuna the great warrior, under the influence of deep distress and ancient is unable to take the correct course of action in the great war of Mahabharata. The war itself and its repercussions send tremors down his spine. He keeps the bow and arrow down in the field of Kurukshetra and refuses to fight. It is at this time that Vishnu incarnated Sri Krishna gives him the beautiful discourse of Gita. The ultimate lines on the fight Principles of Karma, Dharma, Kaam & Moksha, Shri Krishna deals with the neurotic mind of Arjuna and guides him to fulfilment with the treatment and say of Vedic truths.

Many a times this question has arisen that which one book represents the Hindu philosophy. Any religion is philosophy in action. From time to time any ancient philosophy needs intelligent reinterpretations in the content of new changing times and men of wisdom, prophets and seers guide the common man on how to apply effectively the ancient laws in his present life. Thus we are thankful that in the senator Dharma we have had great philosophy and pathfinders who have paved the way with right thinking and right way of life.

The implications of Gita are far beyond religions dedicates and seeps into our day-to-day life. If we imbibe all its teaching in true perspective in the aura of Vedic lore then it clearly explains how action performed without egocentric desire guides and carries forward the mind of its deep seated impressions and makes it purified and mentally prepared for great flights into the infinite Beyond.

Gita is the first guide available in the world which deals in length about the mental problems. The book as a discourse from the God emphasizes that if all our faculties are under control then we can be victorious in the battle of life when mind is not guided by emotions then success is readily achieved.

Mind of any person represents his personality and identifies him as an individual. Mind is defined as the full human being. Mind is identity. As the mind, so is the individual. Whenever the mind of a man is under control then man has full control over all his actions. If the mind is perturbed and distracted then human being is unable to take correct decisions. A strong well balanced mind defines a strong individual.

When we have to define this mind scientifically then the purpose of study and deep understanding we can say that mind constitute two distinct sides—one facing the world of stimuli that it receives from the objects of the world and other facing the within which reacts to the stimuli received.

When we deal with it more scientifically then it is the stimuli from the outer world and its response as a reactor portrayed from the mind within.

In Sanskrit the mind facing the object is called the objective mind and in Sanskrit we call it Alanas and the inward mind is called the subjective mind called Buddhi in Sanskrit.

When the objective and subjective aspects of mind work in unison in any individual then the individual is a whole and healthy one.

In today's scenario anxiety and depressions are increasing. An individual is unable to understand the basic purpose of his existence and the reason why he has come on earth. Thus he falls into the trap of mental illness and his outward performance gets hampered. A individual is whole and healthy in whom the objective and subjective aspects of the mind work in unison and in moments of double, internal conflict, outward aggression, the OBJECTIVE MIND already comes under the decoupling influence of SUBJECTIVE MIND.

For this we have to train our mind in such a way that it has control in the times of turmoil and disturbances. In most of the individuals there is a split between the SUBJECTIVE and OBJECTIVE MIND. This is mainly created by the ignorance of our own identity, our egocentric approach to things, our innate erratic and mostly unfulfilled desires. So much keeps on abusing the untrained and undisciplined mind that the distance between the SUBJECTIVE AND OBJECTIVE MIND increases. The greater the distance between these two aspects of mind, the greater the inner confusion in the individual.

The confusion in the individual about his self worth and about his potentialities leads to self-loathe and self-hatred. The parameter about self awareness and self worth is very low and he tends to fall into the trap of anxiety. The anxious mind is the devil's den and keeps on disturbing all the individual actions of that person.

Gita does not only describe the theory of Karma but explains in detail the scientific explanation of five gyan and the ages of perception. They are described and elaborated in Gita as the gateways of knowledge. Man has well developed receptors organs and during the course of his daily living he is experiencing the outer world through various sensory organs which is known as gyanendriya. We are in a state of constant experience of the outer world, the world of objects around us at all the moments of our wake fullness state. The science has proved it and Gita has explained it very clearly that the innumerable stimuli that react with our sense organs or (receptors) create impulses which reach the objective mind. Science says that these impulses go to the spinal cord and to the brain.

According to the Shrimad Bhagwat Gita the impulse fits deep down to the subjective stratum through the intervening layers of egocentric desires. Any individual born on the earth comes with his own baggage of experiences which cause an effect on the action of the individual. Thus these impulses reaching the SUBJECTIVE MIND OR THE BUDDHI react with the existing impressions of his own past actions that are carefully stored away in the subjective layer and express themselves in the world outside through the five organs of action (effectors).

In the daily chores of living man is meeting with lots of experiences and each experience is a different set of simuli. These stimuli leads to Subjective Mind and adds to the existing layer of impressions already in it either gathered in this life experience or passed on from various past life experiences. Every set of impulses reaching it not only adds to the existing layer of impressions already in it but also gets coloured by the quality of those various hoarded within. These various desires—a list could be of wealth, name, fame, greed, revenge, hatred, love, compassion, fear, etc. influences his actions.

Thus when vasan as stored in the Subjective Mind get translated into action by the impulses received from the sense organs (organs of receptors) then the actions carry a flavour of the existing desires in the Subjective Mind.

The philosophy of Gita emphasized on the theory of clarity of the mind with the purification of body. It emphasizes on the theory of Karma and past like experiences which are accumulated in our SM and are the cause or effect our present Karmas.

Thus every person as long as he is living is going through lot of experiences in his life. Each experience he constantly meets leaves an everlasting impression in his mind.

In the process of perceiving the experiences in the outer world, reacting with the experiences perceived for the outer world, and our actions, all of it unwittingly and unknowingly gets hoarded in the person. Thus in a way the accumulation of dirt in the form of new impressions get added in the SM and the SM gets granulated by the overlapping signatures of our past moments.

The subjective mind or the Buddhi gets increasingly granulated by overlapping signatures of past moments. It is like accumulation of dust over our mind and our ability to perceive the truth gets distorted and influenced in our mind, like the storage bank. The data keeps accumulating and our access to correct data at the right time gets distorted. This prevents us from our quick and active response to things and stimuli. Thus these impressions form a deep wall between the human beings and the super power divinity.

Now if we speak on the terms of scientific theories than the scientist when they comprehend brain they speak of the subconscious mind and the conscious mind.

The conscious mind is one which is awake and responds to the stimuli immediately but the respond to the stimuli is governed by the information, experiences, images, expressions stored in the subconscious mind which is also known as nonconscious mind. Thus many a times our behaviour and response to stimuli is less rationale than we believe to be.

This is because our ability to control thought's synchronize movements—a experience emotions depends on the depth of information processing.

According to level mind model this mind could be divided into:

a) Conscious Mind – It defines all-thought's and actions within our awareness. For e.g. :- smell a aroma of a food being cooked in the kitchen.

b) Subconscious Mind – It defines all reactions and automatic actions we can become aware of if we think about them.

For e.g. :- Our ability to cook, drive, do operations, dare to challenge, sleep etc.

First attempts to synchronize a new set of complex actions are very difficult. They require the involvement of conscious mind but once we become skilled then these movement start to require less conscious awareness until everything begins to flow naturally. All these automatic movements are guided by one of the most powerful inner forces which drive human behaviour— the subconscious mind (also commonly reserved to as the nonconscious mind)

For example :- Our ability to drive a car—once we have learnt how to drive a car we stop thinking which gear to use, when to use acceleration or brake, how to follow the cars and traffic at the back and front.

This is because the skill of driving has settled in our subconscious mind and guides us accordingly.

c) Unconscious Mind – It defines all past events and memories, inaccessible to us no matter how hard we try to remember it

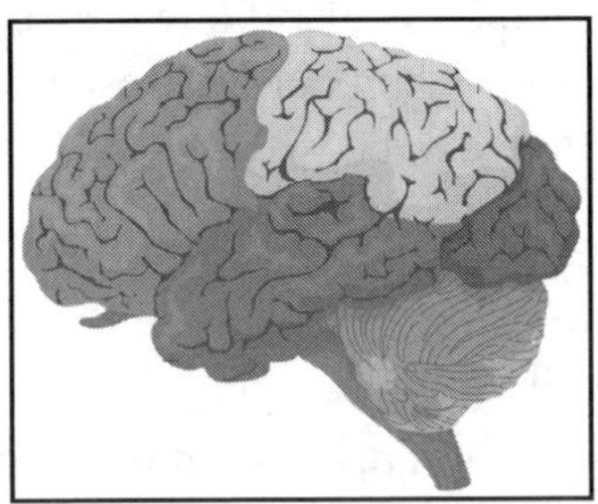

The function of subconscious mind is to store and retrieve data. It's job is to ensure that you respond exactly the way you are programmed. Your subconscious mind makes everything you do say to fit a pattern consistent with your self-concept or your master program. This is why repeating positive affirmations become effective.

One can actually program the mind with positive thoughts and reprogram our thought patterns by slipping in positive and success oriented sound bites. This is subconscious mind which is termed as subjective mind in Shrimad Bhagwat Gita should be filled with motivational quotes, inspirational talk-shows, meeting with people who are positive so that we uplift our own ideas, concepts and thoughts.

Thoughts are electric currents as per science and when they are positive and enhancing our self-worth and self-concept then the subconscious will begin to implement a positive pattern in your way of thinking and our outlook in life.

Though centuries have lapsed from the time Gita was revealed on earth by Shri Krishna that to own the battle field is synonym to the battle of life since time immemorial. It was written great subsequent transformation of thought and experience has taken place. Though much scientific advancement has taken place, human mind has generated new thought ideas and ideals and moved forward, has altered its view point over the agrees, enlarged its thought substance, the basic purpose of these advancements is to render past system of thinking obsolete, or when they are preserved to extend to modify and subtly or visibly to alter their value but still this age old holy text holds relevance in modern times. The Krishna's explanation of the day to day conflict going on in our mind and its practical solution is all what is this text about.

Gita clearly defines the mental state of Arjuna in the war and *Swami Chinmayananda* in his commentary on Gita has defined this state of Arjuna as the Arjuna diseases and the cure offered by Krishna to the ailing mind as Krishna-Cure.

In the context of Arjuna's diseases which even today many individual face on coming in contact with a difficult situation which they are unable to deal with is the manifestations on the physical body with shivering of limbs and recognised symptoms of the maladjustments of his mental level. Infact Shrimad Bhavada Gita is the first medical treatise on neurotic disorder of the brain and metaphysical solutions offered by Shri Krishna to calm the mind.

The Arjuna diseases exhibits that the mind is not only agitated, unsteady and chaotic, but it has lost all its morale. It had arrived to the state of stupor of accepting and recognising superstitious omens portraying disastrous failures and imminent consequences.

31. And I see adverse omens O Keshva. Nor do I see any good in killing my kinsmen in battle.

This same Arjuna disease is faced by many of our students and individual in school and colleges when faced with the challenges and struggles of life. They get into a state of mental confusion and disturbed mind, lents way to emotions that have been totally divorced from their intellect.

The objective mind without the guidance of its subjective aspect runs wild and comes to some unintelligent conclusions.

In the Shrimad Bhagwat Gita—Arjuna wanted victory, he wanted kingdom. He was desirous of worldly pleasures for his egoistic evaluation about himself that he is the greatest hero of all times. Seeing a strong enemy army full of great warriors he suffered anxiety attacks and being desirous of a victorious end of war seemed difficult, his mind got split up.

Looking at the mighty Kaurava forces and the presence of great and eminent warriors of all times he gets into a state of hysteria. He is not able to accept the challenge to fight, his hopes are shattered, his ambition a jolt and his confidence wanes.

Because of his anxious desire for a victorious end of the war, the preoccupation of his mind, dreaming intensively, about the ultimate end of the war brought about a complete divorce between the 'subjective and the 'objective' aspects of his mind.

Later on, we shall discover the various symptoms of this neurotic condition in him and his hysterical blabbering which are typical of such a mental patient. The endeavour in Chapter I of the Gita is to give the complete 'case-history' of a patient suffering from the typical 'Arjuna disease'. The Bhagwat Gita gives, as emphasized clearly by Swami Chinmayananda, an extremely efficient 'Krishna-cure' for this soul-killing 'Arjuna disease'.

Arjuna said:

Seeing these my kinsmen, O Krishna, arrayed, eager to fight,

My limbs fail and my mouth is parched, my body quivers and my hair stand on end.

कृपया परयाविष्टो विषीदन्निदमब्रवीत् ।

krpaya parayavisto visidannidamabravit

अर्जुन उवाच—

दृष्ट्वेमं स्वजनं कृष्ण युयुत्सुं समुपस्थितम् ॥ २८ ॥

arjuna uodca
drstvemam svajanam krsna yuyutsum samupasthitam 28.

सीदन्ति मम गात्राणि मुखं च परिशुष्यति ।
वेपथुश्च शरीरे मे रोमहर्षश्च जायते ॥ २९ ॥

sidanti mama gatrani mukhai ca parisusyati
vepathusca sarire me romaharṣasca jayate 29.

In these two stanzas, there is an exhaustive enumeration of the symptoms that the patient could then recognise in his own physical body as a result of his mental confusion. That which Sanjaya had glorified as 'pity', when coming out of Arjuna's own mouth, gains a more realistic expression. Arjuna says "seeing my kinsmen gathered here anxiously determined to fight, my limbs shiver" etc.

All these symptoms are described in the textbooks of modern psychology as typical symptoms of the mental disease named 'anxiety-neurosis'.

The Gandiva-bow slips from my hand and my skin burns all over: I am also unable to stand and my mind is whirling round, as it were.

Here Arjuna is adding some more details of the symptoms of his disease. Earlier we had a list of symptoms that manifested on the physical body. Now in this stanza, Arjuna tries to report recognised-symptoms of the maladjustments at his mental level.

Not only is his mind unsteady, agitated and chaotic, but it has lost all its morale. It has come down to the stupid level of accepting and recognising superstitious omens portending disastrous failures and imminent consequences.

गाण्डीवं स्रंन्सते हस्तात्त्वक्चैव परिदह्यते ।
न च शक्नोम्यवस्थातुं भ्रमतीव च मे मनः ॥ ३० ॥

gandivam sramsate hastattvakcaiva paridahyate na ca saknomyavasthatum bhramativa ca me manah 30.

Not only does the following stanza vividly picture to us his mental confusions, but it also shows how far his discrimination has been drained off, and his morale destroyed.

31. And I see adverse omens, O Keshava. Nor do I see any good in killing my kinsmen in battle.

In this state of mental confusion, when his emotions have been totally divorced from his intellect, the "objective-mind", without the guidance of its 'subjective-aspect', runs wild and comes to some unintelligent conclusions. He says, "I desire neither victory, nor empire, nor even pleasure". It is a recognised fact that a patient of hysteria, when allowed to talk, will, in a negative way, express the very cause for the attack. For example, when a woman, hysterically raving, repeatedly declares with all emphasis, that she is not tired of her husband that she still respects him, that he still loves her, that there is no rupture between them, etc., she, by these very words, clearly indicates the exact cause of her mental chaos.

Similarly, the very denials of Arjuna clearly indicate to all careful readers how and why he got into such a state of mental grief. He desired victory. He urgently wanted the kingdom. He anxiously expected to win pleasures for himself and his relations. But the challenging look of the mighty Kaurava forces and the great and eminent warriors standing ready to fight, shattered hopes, blasted his ambitions, and undermined his self-confidence and he slowly developed the well-known 'Arjuna-disease', the cure for which is the theme of the Gita.

निमित्तानि च पश्यामि विपरीतानि केशव।

न च श्रेयोऽनुपश्यामि हत्वा स्वजनमाहवे ॥ ३१ ॥

nimittani ca pasyami viparitani kesava na ca sreyo'nupasyami hatva svajanamáhave 31.

The same happens with our students, they face Arjuna disease syndrome when faced with the challenges of life. Their all strength, decision making capacity and self-confidence suffers and seeing their egocentric, ambition suffering a jolt they go into the pangs of anxiety and depression and sometimes unable to sooth their ambition gives into their fears and commit suicide.

The beginning of the discourse between Arjuna and Shri Krishna is over the advisability of the Dharmayudha. Here according to Shri Chinmayananda-

When Arjuna gets no moral support or word of encouragement from his friend Krishna then he says

Arjuna declares with a mock sprit of renunciation that he had so much large heartedness in him that he would not kill his cousins, even if they were to kill him.

An understatement to say that it infact it is the first book of psychiatry and psychological counselling existing in the world. Thus it is very useful in giving a deeper insight into the mental anxiety faced by the students and best part it offers hands on solutions to cure that anxiety.

The Behaviour of a super hero Arjuna at the battlefield was a startling awareness in realm of Psychology. Arjuna syndrome and Krishna's lecture are a treatise of modern day Psychology, in fact the complete Shrimad Bhagwat Gita is a scientific lecture on Psychology.

Thus we sea that in our day-to-day life we are facing so many outwardly experiences and these experiences are getting accumulated in the mindset of individuals. Shrimad Bhagwat Gita clearly says that an individual should live his/her own destiny perfectly than to live an imitation of somebody's else... Repression of thoughts and actions have a neurotic effect on an individual and hence we should refrain from it.

In school, children are taught to be quiet meek spectators and followers in the growing up process, they are never allowed to speak up their minds. The intuitiveness and awareness to understanding things is crushed in the start itself. Thus slowly the repressive mind and subdued expressions find its opening in abnormal behaviour of the individual later on in life.

We have to learn to make this believe in the child that he has to learn to respect time, himself/ herself as he/she is important and not to judge oneself with the eyes of the world.

We have to teach our children to fight the expectations of the world, family and friends. A learner has to be taught very early in life that he/she should not place to much expectation on self too. These battles fought are battles won. Slowly when we learn to overcome our own fears, short comings and weaknesses, success will greet us with open arms.

❑

Chapter-3

एवमुक्त्वाऽर्जुनः सङ्ख्ये रथोपस्थउपाविशत् ।
विसृज्य सशरंचापं शोकसंविग्नमानसः ।।

EVAMUKTVAA ARJUNAH SANKHYE
RATHOPASTHA UPAAVISHAD
VISRUJYA SASHARAM CHAAPAM
SHOKA SAMVIGNA MAANASAH

Having said, in battlefield no,
In chariot he dropped low;
Leaving bow and arrow,
He grieved with sorrow.

In our country with the decline of Gurukul culture and emergence of commercial schools, examination at every step has become a challenge for a seeker.

Since childhood, every seeker of education (child) is made to face tough competitions for entry into schools, colleges, universities, career and so on.

This challenge many a times creates doubts in the minds of learners or seekers. Most of the time many get drowned in the fear of possible disaster. This impending defeat takes away from them the spirit to work or perform to the best of their capabilities.

We see so many bright students in conflict with themselves. They are unable to evaluate their strengths and focus only on their weaknesses.

They are more caught in failures than in performance. More caught in self-defeat and shame of withdrawal than in action.

Having said in battlefield no,
In chariot he dropped low,
Leaving bow and arrow,
He grieved with sorrow.

We see a perfect case of this during Mahabharata where Arjuna laid his bow and arrow in front of Lord Krishna. He was so much shaken that he could not gather courage to fight.

Our lives is a battlefield and we all are warriors in this journey. At every step we have to fight and prove our ability. Various vices like lack of preparation, dedication, loss of focus, fear of failure, shame of withdrawal, ridicule of society stands in our path of excellence.

The same situation which Arjuna faced in Mahabharata arise in our lives at every step. Our self-doubt of our own capabilities and potential, coupled with fear of losing, pulls us down. The end result is that a learner or a seeker of education forgets his goals and withdraws in total helplessness.

This is the time when an informed teacher should guide the learner with informed knowledge.

This is the time when Lord Krishna came in as a spiritual and moral guide and uttered such words which removed the darkness which had engulfed the seeker – Arjuna.

कर्मण्येवाधिकारस्ते मा फलेषु कदाचन
मां कर्मफलहेतूर्भूर्मा ते संगोऽस्त्वकर्मणि

Thus, we see that Krishna guides Arjuna to do selfless work. Only work is under our control. Karma is the centered point in our lives.

Thus as students we should study and should not grieve in sorrow. Wherever there is doubt in studies we should get it cleared and be focused on our path and goal without tension.

This is the path of self-evaluation and self-actualisation. Thus, the role of a good teacher is to be the motivator and guide. He should remove the darkness engulfed in the minds of the seeker and guide him towards enlightenment.

तमसो मा ज्योर्तिगमय

Growing means that we should realize our hidden and infinite energy and should release it to achieve our goals and dreams.

If we take on the challenges of the world with all our might and strength then success, sooner or later is bound to follow. Life is all about moving from darkness to light, mortality to immortality. We as souls with divinity vested in us and are become immortal beings, when our acts are pious and for the larger benefit of society. The reading of this great scripture teaches us to rise in life and learn to achieve our inner potentials for our betterment.

At every step in this Holy Text Krishna ignites the inner spark in the Arjuna to become attuned to his own energy and strength.

This is what we have to practice with our youth. Through proper counseling and teaching we have to create the sparks in him/her to achieve his/her real worth, and will all the battles of life with fearlessness. Challenges come and challenges go, the victory lies in doing our karmas with full commitment.

❑

Chapter-4

तं तथा कृपयाऽविष्ठमश्रुपूर्णाकुलेक्षणम् ।
विषीदन्तमिदं वाक्यमुवाच मधुसूदनः ॥

कुतस्त्वा कश्मलमिदं विषमे समुपस्थितम् ।
अनार्यजुष्टमस्वर्ग्यम् अकीर्तिकरमर्जुन ॥

TAM TATHAA KRIPAYAAVISHTAA
ASHRU POORNA KULEKSHANAM
VISHEEDANTAMIDAM VAAKYAM
UVAACHA MADHUSUDANAH
KUTASTAVAA KASHMALAMIDAM
VISHAMEY SAMUPASTHITHAM
ANAARYA JUSHTAM ASWARGYAM
AKEERTI KARAMARJUNA

With kindness in heart,
and with tears which hurt;
when Arjun was a mess,
Madhusudan said this.

Dejection is a cage,
At this critical stage;
From whence it came,
Arjun! is it not a shame?

Our very own philosophy speaks of moving from darkness to light and from bondage to liberation.

Here, liberation is not only Moksha in its very essence but, it is liberation from the bondage of depression, sorrow, doubts, fears and failures. Easily said, but not easily accomplished for, we all are imprisoned in our own personality and thought process, build up by our own present and past life experiences.

When we are born, we come with our baggage of learning and a set pattern of our thinking.

In the utter state of frustration and helplessness a responsible Guru holds the hand of the Shishya and guides him to the right path.

The Lord revealed his true self to the seeker Arjuna at the battlefield and motivated him for action. With his infinite illumination, he removed the darkness surrounding Arjuna. He told Arjuna that you are just a part of me so fear not and move forward to achieve your goal. In this battlefield, the goal of Arjuna was victory over evil.

In a similar way, in all our battlefields, the Guru with the grace of God (the infinite) guides the learners and removes the darkness which is surrounding the seeker. It is the darkness of not realizing that the seeker is a small part of the infinite and has the potential to achieve the impossible. The seeker restricts the energy and stops growing.

This awakening has to be made by the able and firm hands of the Guru—an all encompassing, compassionate impersonification of God.

What is good the Guru who can not guide and motivate his own Shishya?

In today's education system we see so much of frustration writ large on the forehead of the Guru. He feels incapacitated to act as a motivator and guide. For that the Guru himself has to feel the divine bliss in himself and perform his duties selflessly and with the sole objective of bringing out the best in the Shishya.

Yesteryear Guru's took the responsibility of the Shishya in their fold and tried to bring out the best in them. Thus today's teachers or Gurus should learn to start taking responsibility for their own conduct and the conduct of their Shishyas and bring out the best in their students. This is possible only when teacher himself rises from the biases and bondages and takes upon himself the role of monitoring and guiding the seeker towards educational salvation.

The teacher-student bondage should be such that student as seeker of knowledge is able to share all his/her fears, emotional disturbances, weakness and failures with the teacher as mentor.

Since, with the vast treasure of knowledge and experiences of teaching, he is able to address all the emotional disturbances and educational defects of the students with a firm but caring hand. The teacher is like a doctor, where compassion is the key to success. No learner can stand dejection and especially from his Guru whom he sees as a human embodiment of God.

A responsible teacher takes the situation in hand and takes out his student from the darkness of depression, dejection, fear, insecurities and failure. The insecurities should be addressed at the earliest by a teacher in a convincing and caring way to get out the best possible results.

A responsible teacher with his vast set of experience lifts the student from darkness to light. The responsible teacher illuminates the light inside the seeker just like Krishna did at the battlefield addressed all the insecurities of the Arjuna and enlightened him to the path of light and decision-making.

Insecurities arise when decision-making capacity is lost in the seeker and he is seeping low in the pond of indecisiveness, leading to insecurities and thus depression.

A learner who was born to realize his inner light and take it to the path of perfection is caught in the mirage of dejection. It is here that an informed learned compassionate teacher helps the seeker in realizing his inner-worth and guides him away from that darkness or depression for which a learner was not born.

These things are caused by overreaction to external factors and the negative external factors should be avoided as far as possible.

Thus an informed involved responsible teacher breaks the bondage of depression and leads the learner to liberation and this is possible by being connected with the seeker like, Madhav was with Partha at the battlefield of Kurukshetra.

❑

Chapter-5

क्लैब्यं मा स्म गमः पार्थ नैतत्त्वय्युपपद्यते।
क्षुद्रं हृदयदौर्बल्यं त्यक्त्वोत्तिष्ठ परन्तप॥

KLAIBYAM MA SMA GAMAH PAARTHA
NAITATTVA YYUPA PADYATE
KSHUDRAM HRIDAYA DAURBALYAM
TYAKTOTTISHTA PARANTAPAH

Yield not Partha to weakness, this,
it is not fit to be feeble like this
weakness of heart is low, unwise
"Terror of enemies"! Get up and rise!

Many a times it is a very common practice that a learner becomes caught in the web of weakness. This is because the external expectations are too high on him (his parents, school, peer, society) that he is afraid to take on the world with full commitment. His own mental preparedness is not sufficient enough to face the external challenges. He gets depressed and disturbed.

This is the time when a committed Guru comes in handy to elevate him from the bondage of darkness.

These days there is much talk about EQ/IQ. EQ is the Emotional Quotient of a child and is related to the emotional connectivity of the child with his immediate environment.

It is the disturbance at this level which hampers the growth of child. The emotional preparedness for facing the world is the key to success. It is here that a Guru comes in handy and slowly but firmly helps the learner to overcome his weakness.

This is achieved by constantly initiating the thinking process of the learner. Many a times it so happens that emotional conduct is overruling the rational and correct thinking of the learner. Thus the seeker of education is not able to focus correctly and with concentration on the objective and purpose for which the education is sought.

It is at this time that a good responsible teacher awakens the inner strength of the learner, makes him realize his true worth and potentiality and guides him towards perfection.

The all encompassing Mahabharata Yudh was in a very critical situation which Arjuna was facing. He had all his near and dear ones standing in the battlefield and he had to fight them out. His emotions overruled his karma or action.

Hence, Krishna the Lord, as a spiritual head awakened the purpose inside him, guided him on the path of Dharma and asked him to fulfil his duties selflessly.

Arjuna underestimated his real worth in the battle-field but like an inspiring teacher, “Mukund-the all Prevailing” reminded him of his capabilities, past success and achievements.

He makes Partha realize his inner strength and potentiality so that he stops underestimating his own self.

Most of the time depression occurs because we fear that external situation is far, too tough and beyond our control. Our own lack of inner preparedness stops us from fighting it out and finding a solution. It is at this time that there is a need of an emotional Guru, who makes us see the situation with full clarity and helps us in fighting it out.

Our very own Krishna in the form of human embodiment as Guru comes as spiritual healer and guides us through. We become like small treasure of potentialities and are able to handle the situation with full force.

We are the small God's—his very own creation.

Thus, we see that even small encouragement comes in handy at the time of depressing situation. Encouragement illuminates our inner light and energises us forward.

Encouragement is the key to building our confidence and determination.

❑

Chapter-6

कार्पण्यदोषोपहतस्वभावः पृच्छामि त्वां धर्मसम्मूढचेताः।
यच्छ्रेयः स्यान्निश्चितंब्रूहि तन्मे शिष्यस्तेऽहं
शाधि मां त्वां प्रपन्नम्।।

अशोच्यानन्वशोचस्त्वं प्रज्ञावादांश्च भाषसे।
गतासूनगतासूंश्च नानुशोचन्ति पण्डिताः।।

KARPANYA DOSHOPA HATA SWABHAAVAH
PRUCHAAMI TWAAM DHARMA SAMMOODHA CHETAH
YATSHREYA SANNISCHITAM BROOHI TANME
SIHSHYASTE AHAM SHAADHI MAAMTVAAM PRAPANNAM

ASHOCHAYAA NANVA SHOCHASTVAM
PRAGNAA VAADAANSCHA BHAASHASE
GATAASU NA GATTSUNSCHA
NAANU SHOCHATI PANDITAAH

It is not clear what should I do,
what is right, too, I don't know,
please show the path I come to you,
Tell me Master! which way to go.

You grieve for which none should grieve,
on the top of that logic you give,
for those who left and didn't leave,
see my friend! wise never grieve.

In our ancient Gurukul system, a Guru and his wife Gurumata became the guardians of the learner during his education period. The learner also accepted his Guru as his family and did all sorts of job for the family. This system helped in building a strong bondage between the Guru and his Shishya (learner).

This bondage cleared all misgivings between the Guru and his learner. Our epic Ramayana says that Ramchandraji broke the Lord Shiva's bow and married Sita when he was with his Guru. Thus Guru was the family of the Shishya and any tension which arose was very clearly shared with the Guru.

Those students who were genuine and keen took advantage of this situation and used their stay to clear all their doubts with the Guru. They served the Guru and got emotional security in return.

The students because of this bondage had trust with the Guru and shared openly their thoughts. Many a times a learner lost his clarity and got tense, then the teacher guided him to the right path.

It's a learner with lack of experience and the requisite knowledge who is in difficulty to take clear decision. In today's scenario with commercialization of education system, students as learners have lost all respect for their teachers. Then see in themselves a far realized goal of clearing competitions and see their Guru as mere teachers in their path of success. The human bondage is totally lacking.

The push and pull of the situation and the insecurity which arises out of it causes confusion. He starts worrying of what has happened and what could happen. It is at this time that a responsible teacher brings the learner to the present reality.

Usually the worries and tensions are caused by the logic and belief of the learners. This logic and belief is developed because of the preconceived notion a learner brings to from his previous background. Hence each learner is different. This logic has to be cleared and by the able hands of the Guru a new clarity and logic has to be developed in the learner.

This new clarity which is developed in the learner helps him to see beyond the logic and enables him to be wise to face the present situation in reality.

This helps the learner to face the problem and focus clearly on the solutions. A confused learner sinks deeper in the situation and broods over the problem but a wise Guru shows him the path and makes him reach a logical solution.

Many a times we brood over the past and come under pressure. The bad situations of the past creates such a mark on our personality that we are not able to move ahead with clarity. A good responsible teacher, understands the confusion which is going on in the minds of his learner and guides him towards the correct path.

The moment the confused depressed mind of the Partha asks, “My future is all disturbed. I don’t know what to do. Guide me” and like Kanha guided Arjuna in the battlefield, in the same way Guru guides him to his goal.

Thus, we see that the Guru is aware of the situation and its solutions. This is because Guru has more knowledge, understanding of the situation, higher level of expertise to handle the situation well. His bonding and influence on the learner is also well developed. Hence, he is in a position to guide his student and lead him out of trauma and conflict. The learner should develop a trustable bond with his Guru to be successful.

Guru is the guiding light in the Shishya. Guru is the pillar of strength.

❑

Chapter-7

मात्रास्पर्शास्तुकौन्तेय शीतोष्णसुखदुः खदाः।
आगमापायिनोऽनित्यास्तांस्तितिक्षस्व भारत।।

MAATRAA SPARSHASTU KAUNTEYA
SHEETOSHNA SUKHA DUKHADAA
AGAMAAPAYIONO ANITYA
TAAM STITHIKSHASVA BHARATA

Heat and cold, pleasure and pain,
Contact the senses again and again;
Impermanent they come and go,
Bear them Bhaarata! considering then so.

It has been always quoted and found to be true that nothing in life is permanent. Life itself is a constant changing scene, happiness follows sorrow, day follows night and vice versa. Nothing in life is permanent hence it becomes the responsibility of a good learner to see the inner preparedness for all the situations. That is why in old days even the children of rich and poor alike spent their childhood in the hermitage of their Guru preparing themselves for the adversities in future. Education in yesteryears was such that it prepared the learner more internally than for external gains. A seeker was made well versed in all the crafts. The life of a young student was tough, disciplined and full of hard work. It was equal for rich and poor. Even the children of Kings and Prince did all the chores which made them tough from inside. They sat on the throne with mint and aptitude. Today we offer all the comfort to our children in the guise of taking care.

The pursuit of education was more for spiritual pursuit than for economical gains. Hence, during the course of education every learner was supposed to become tough from inside and education looked deeply into character building more than the material pursuits.

Such should be the course of education even today under the able guidance of a Guru that a learner becomes strong and focused internally to face the tough times outside.

Depression and tension occurs when a learner feels that the present situation is out of control and will last forever. The future holds no promises, everything is lost, and the learner falls in the trap of hopelessness which adds to frustration in him. This happens because his inner preparation for adversity is not well taken care of.

We see that family and teachers have lost the bondage with the learner. In time of adversity he is not able to confide in them because of lack of trust and confidence that he will be understood in the right perspective. Hence he/she falls in the trap of wrong advice.

Thus a good teacher awakens the potentiality in the learner and tells him that life is a cycle of gains and losses.

The learner should not brood on the loses but instead should gather the courage and awaken to the inner strength and follow the path of hard work, dedication and righteousness to achieve his goal.

In tough times, one should remain focused and remove all doubts which surround the learner and should plunge forward with full strength, vigour and preparedness.

It so happens that, as young students, the school education system does not prepare a child for mental adversities, difficulties and struggles. Education itself is thought of as malady to all ills. Hence, when adversities surround us we become desperate and not in a position to cope will the challenges. Life skills is missing from an education system.

The insight into the lives of many a successful people, who have achieved it after going through many failures, defeat and in great adversities should act as an inspiration for the young learner.

The Guru motivates the young learner to take on new adventures, do new experiments in odd situations and to be able to be more focussed and in the capacity of a decision-maker. This happens when learner takes decision as a young aspirant.

Most of the time, darkness surrounds, as the young learner is not able to take a right decision and hence a right step. Rote learning takes away the pleasure from learning.

A responsible Guru encourages him to take many small decisions to be able to take on a long leap and plunge in life. No decision is a wrong decision. Many a times decision doesn't succeed because of many internal and external factors and thus a good teacher motivates, guides and promotes his Shishya towards decision making and holds on to him till he succeeds. Decision making and taking the onus and responsibility for a wrong decision is a step towards success.

Once a child is able to be in a position to take decision, he will bear the responsibility for his actions. He will fight out his own failures and get focused towards success.

Krishna tells Kauntey that, nothing in this world is permanent. Neither heat nor cold, nor success or failure, neither name and fame. Everything is bound to finish hence one should just get focused and fight out one's own weaknesses and failures and move on in life. Life is given to us to enjoy varied experiences and to arrive at concrete personality building lesson. Suppose if we spend a lot of money then many a times situations would be so placed that because of wastage of money we are facing economic deprivation. Such situation will prevail till we learn to be prudent with money. It is a marvel of human existence that in spite of so much sorrow and sufferings we learn to survive. This survival instinct and moving on makes a person great. Hence very early in life, we should have inner-preparedness for taking informed decisions. Inertia and Inaction are disastrous for growth and success.

❑

Chapter-8

अथ चेत्त्वमिमं धर्म्यं संग्रामं न करिष्यसि।
ततः स्वधर्मं कीर्तिं च हित्वा पापमवाप्स्यसि।।
अकीर्तिंचापिभूतानि कथयिष्यन्ति तेऽव्ययाम्।
संभावितस्य चाकीर्तिर्मरणादतिरिच्यते।।

ATHA CHET TVAM IMAM DHARMYAM
SANGRAAMAM NA KARISHYASI
TATAH SWADHARMAM KEERTINCHA
HITVAA PAAPAM AVAAPSYASI

AKEERTISCHAPI BHOOTAANI
KATHAYSHYANTI TE AVYAYAAM
SAMBHAVITASCHA CHA AKEERTI
MARANAAD ATI RICHYATE

If you do not fight this war,
Partha! see the right war;
The dutifulness and your fame,
Both will cease, so your name.

Future people will surely tell,
Infamously how you fell;
For a gentleman, let me tell,
That is more than death also hell.

Life even in day-to-day is a battle. We are battling with our emotions, our defeats, our sorrows, our illness, our misfortunes but most of us have the spirit to go on.

Hence, a good responsible teacher awakens the spirit of warrior in the learner and ask him to face the situation with full preparedness rather than running away from it.

When we fight our battle, there are chances of winning but, in plainly running away there is a clear-cut defeat.

So, a good responsible teacher would never want his learner to succumb to defeat so easily. Running away from a situation is a sure cut sign of a loser. So, a Guru guides his learner to fight in a similar way, Banke Bihari asked Arjuna to keep away all weaknesses and face the battlefield with full courage.

If the learner leaves the battlefield, then he or she earns bad name. So the spirit of a warrior should always be present in the learner.

An encouraging teacher motivates the learner to move from mortality to immortality by overcoming the adverse situation and accepting the challenge with full confidence.

A responsible teacher helps the learner overcome the problem and the critical situation he is caught with.

A responsible teacher cheers up the moral of the learner in such a way that instead of sulking in indecisiveness, the learner focuses on solutions and fight out all the odds. Giving up is defeat and fighting back is success. For, when we fight back, we use all our strength with the intent of winning and giving our enemy defeat. In order to fight back we use all the strategies to overcome defeat and this slowly leads us to success, name, fame and glory.

The difficulty comes in the path of every person. No success can be achieved without hard work and dedication, commitment, and a focused attitude. Hence, a Guru sees to it that his learner is not getting trapped in a critical situation and shows him the path to success.

The Madhusudan guides Partha out of the critical situation in Mahabharata. He guides him that if he does not participate in the war, then he has already lost half the battle and brought disrepute to himself and his family. Thus, a good warrior fights with total vigor and force not worrying about the consequences.

We are only entitled to our karma and deeds and should not unnecessary worry about the results.

Thus, the advice of Krishna in Gita is to face the situation squarely and forget the consequences of our karmas. Only karma is in our hand and result of factors overshadowed in darkness.

Krishna advice Arjuna that when you do not fight, you will bring disrepute to your family and ill-name for yourself. This facing and fighting the salvation and coming out of it is the biggest victory.

In today's scenario our learners should fight all the odds occurring in their lives as experiences. The odds could be hostile family situations, lack of resources, ineffective working conditions, failed opportunities, no support system, economic deprivation, lack of knowledge etc. Inspite of all the odds we still have one chance to fight back and win. So, a Guru should guide him to fight against all odds and achieve success.

Running from a situation is cowardice and disastrous. Fighting back has chances of victory.

❑

Chapter-9

व्यवसायत्मिका बुद्धिरेकेह कुरुनन्दन।
बहुशाखा ह्यनन्ताश्चबुद्धयोऽव्यवसायिनाम्।।

VYVAVASAAYATMIKAA BUDDHI
EKHEA KURUNANDANA
BAHU SHAAKHAAHI ANANTAASCHA
BUDDHAYO AVYAVASAYINAAM

Intellect of endeavouring one,
Single and firm, Oh! Kunti's son,
Intellect of the wavering one,
Runs many ways end is none.

एक साधे सब सधे
सब साधे सब जाये

In life at the Gurukul stage, an informed teacher guides the learner towards fixed goals. In our ancient times, Guru recognized the potentiality of the learner and guided him through, like Dronacharya guided Arjuna into archery and henceforth.

Even today a teacher is quick to notice the potentiality of the child and guides him towards indentifying his goal. Teacher motivates the student towards his goal.

When a critical situation arises, then a child/learner gets confused as to what to do. Lot of doubts and insecurities arises in his mind and he is unable to focus properly and identify his goal in life.

This is a time when an informed teacher comes in handy and guides the student towards perfection.

The goal which is marred in non-clarity is slowly cleared and he is able to move forward with single minded determination.

Our clarity and thought process is disturbed during growing up age. This is the time when we are unable to focus and find out ways to our future. Thus the able hand of a good teacher guides the child and focuses him towards his goals. It is encouragement which is needed at the time of crisis which guides the learner forward.

Youth is the time when a child is growing physically but is also learning to assert his personality and recognizing his ego. His self identity and centrism is making a mark in his growth. This is the same time he is opening up to the outer world and peer pressure has started playing a strong influence on the learner. The distractions of outer world and the inner conflict to lay focused starts playing in his life. Hence the need arises for a good teacher.

There are lot of mental disturbances when life goes through a rough phase. There is a struggle to keep our morale high, our attention focused and not succumb to sorrows and frustrations. It is exactly the time when need for aware person who can cast positive influence in our live is needed by us.

A good informed teacher helps us in making our resolution firm and sticking to it. It helps in moving forward.

It is not easy for a person in a difficult situation not to waiver and get disturbed. It is but human to get carried away in a traumatic situation. But a good teacher helps us see the right path and focuses us towards clarity.

A good teacher guides the intellect towards aim, purpose and goal and motivates the learner to achieve it through full commitment.

Thus the need for a good teacher in difficult times become nonetheless important.

Crisis does not come informing us. It is a sudden and strong thus and we are in a trap of struggle. It becomes very important to maintain our cool and find our solutions rather than curse ourselves and brood over the problem.

Guidance and strong support helps us a long way.

It helps us with strong determination and focused aim.

❑

Chapter-10

यावानर्थ उदपाने सर्वतः संप्लुतोदके।
तावान्सर्वेषु वेदेषु ब्राह्मणस्य विजानतः।।

YAVAANARTHA UDAPAANE
SARVATA SAMPLUTODAKE
TAAVAAN SARVESHU VEDESHU
BRAAHMANASYA VIJAANATAH

When clear water, in the river, flow well,
What is the use of water in the well,
Vedas, scriptures are like that,
For knower of ultimate, who knows 'THAT'

In our country, which boast of an age, old tradition, the Guru is the embodiment of God. He is bestowed with the power of creation and changing the destinies of its learner. Guru could be in the form of mother, father or teacher. The first two hold prime position in the lives of a learner for they are the first Guru's a learner interacts with.

When a child is of attainable age then the role of teacher takes a centerstage. The Guru-Shishya parampara in our country is a continuation of this role a teacher has to take when a child is of a considerable age when his awareness is becoming awakened and he is moving beyond gaining communicative skills. At this stage a child is awakened to his potentialities internally as well as externally. Thus, the choice of a Guru and the role he adopts in the lives of a learner becomes of prime importance.

A nation is what—it's Guru's chart it out for it. A whole generation is moulded by the influence of a Guru hence, the importance of Guru at any stage cannot be undermined.

In the battlefield of Kurukshetra, Krishna as a God, adopts the role of a Guru and awakens the inner-self of his learner, Kaunteya. Thus, the relevance of Gita for guiding the learners thus becomes of prime importance.

Gita is the first available treatise where mental health of an individual and its importance in the lives of individuals and its influence on society is discussed at great length. Such a book is not found in any part of the world dealing with mental health and solution elaborated to this extent towards self and surrounding.

Krishna through his teachings in Gita tries to awaken the divinity in his Shishya. He guides him to delearn and then to relearn about new heights. Gita says that at every stage we are having new experience and new inferences are found from them. These inferences define our actions and actions define reactions. It is a cyclic process. He guides Kaunteya to move ahead from his archery skills and achieve the very purpose of his life. This essence and philosophy of Gita is the centerstage of learning process in any education system.

The irony is that in our schools we are focusing only on bookish knowledge and not awakening the spark in our learners to explore and experiment. We are not allowing them to take the control of their lives in their own hands, awaken the spark within them. In the guise of education we are stopping them to enjoy and unravel the mysterious nature.

A good responsible teacher is one such person who is a river of knowledge, information, ideas and creativity. Since he is self realized, he can guide his learner to that level of realization. Thus the need of a good Guru becomes all the more important in today's scenario.

A good teacher acts like mentor and guide and his role is not only of passing on the information but to encourage the learner to the path of self study and self actualization.

When a teacher takes his profession with passion then the student starts taking education seriously. It is like a Midas touch —the seriousness of the Guru passes on to the Shishya.

This is not attained in a day. For a teacher to become a Guru one has to continuously move inwards, awaken himself to the immense and vast sea of knowledge which is present all around.

Then only a teacher can reach the level of a Guru.

The Guru should become all encompassing and should have such capacity that it can pull the student towards himself.

His flow of knowledge should bath the student in its water and the divine connection passes on from Guru to the Shishya. In order to influence Arjuna in the battlefield, Krishna reveals the divine self. Guru has to himself be a seeker of knowledge and delve in the philosophical questions of self, surroundings and the physical and metaphysical world. Guru has to rise from an ordinary teacher to a divine being. Easily said but difficult in practice. For the day Guru has to himself be a seeker of knowledge and dedicated towards proper mental growth of his Shishya, the whole society would be changing for the betterment.

❑

Chapter-11

कर्मण्येवाधिकारस्ते मा फलेषु कदाचन।
मा कर्मफलहेतूर्भूर्मा ते सङ्गोऽस्त्वकर्मणि।।

KARMANIYEVADHIKAARASTE
MAA PHALESHU KADAACHANA
MAA KARMA PHALA HETURBHU
MAA TE SANGOTSVA AKARMANI

Only for work you have right,
Fruits of the work are not your right,
Cause for fruits you become not,
In not doing the work be interested not.

The whole theory of Gita is Karma and its fruits. Gita lays emphasis on the doctrine that one should continue doing selfless karma in order to progress in life and achieve the ultimate purpose of life.

This doctrine could very well be inculcated in an aspiring child/learner by helping and guiding him to this doctrine in principle. This could be well illustrated through the ideals a good responsible teacher presents to his learner.

When a learner gets focused on the principle of working hard with dedication, hard work, moving towards self studies and self actualization, then he can very easily transform his skills and abilities into success. His hard work leads him to fruitful results.

This habit of hard work and discipline is best inculcated at the childhood level.

A good inspiring teacher through dedication and meticulous work sets an example for the learners to follow. When we are hard working then we can overcome many difficulties and travel the ocean of life (Bhavsagar ke Paar).

It is our hard work which adds value to our lives and we can achieve our ultimate purpose in life.

Krishna in Gita guides Partha to selfless work without bothering for its fruits. The same doctrine applies to young learner that without bothering about marks, position, credit and fame, he should study, dedicate himself to improve his skills, learning new craft and moving towards perfection.

The selfless work of the learner will help him in enhancing his skills and ultimately success is bound to come.

In today's scenario, parents and teachers do not motivate the learner towards learning. They guide the child towards learning to achieve marks. The end result is that most of the learners do not work in the direction of gaining perfection. They study for marks which are very superfluous. Even education being imparted in schools is half backed and not up to the mark. These days depression and frustration is becoming centerstage of many individuals, lives. It is so, because we are not deriving pleasure out of our work, we are simply working to achieve superfluous external gains like money, position, name and fame. The moment we don't get it we are devastated.

Further, when during the course of our studies we are directed towards its fruits, we cannot attain the best results. For the mind is not fully concentrated and is divided for the results. This adds to anxiety, nervousness and finally to depression.

If the learner is committed enough to only learn, then he will gain better knowledge and will put it to better use and hence achieve better results.

In a school setup and scenario, a teacher who is dedicated towards his work, acts as an inspiration for many learners and guides the learner towards perfection. Perfection in concepts and theories is the key to learning. It helps us in building our own concepts and inferences and hence might contribute to the world by giving our own interpretations.

For young learners, their teacher is their ultimate guide and mentor and they follow the traits and personality of their Guru.

Thus, the personality of the Guru should be so much committed towards his own discipline and conduct so upright that learner follows on the footprint of his Guru. This helps in inculcating good moral values in the learner and building up his personality.

The conduct of the learner is the reflection of his Guru. Hence a teacher who is workaholic guides his Shishya to be so.

In this life we have come only to work and strive towards perfection. The principle of Karma is the cardinal point in human existence.

This could be best achieved if we get into the habit of learning to work very early in our lives.

Perfection is achieved only through self study and hard works and this discipline has to be inculcated in the child as early as possible.

When we work aimlessly and selflessly, then work becomes worship and its fruits are divine blessings.

Around us we see everyone working, gardener is taking care of its plants, farmer of its farm, sun and moon are working and so is mother earth. The nature has given us birth to work.

They all are working day in and day out to keep us safe and happy. So we should also follow the same suit.

Then why can't a learner as a student study hard to learn and excel his/her potentialities. It is only work which can transform our own skills and abilities into perfection. Only work yields results and transform our dream into realities.

A good teacher is himself a dedicated lot. From morning to dusk a teacher is working hard to enhance his own skills and pass it on to the learner. No perfection in a learner would be achieved unless and until an able guidance of a teacher is present.

An able teacher guides the learner to focus on studies and learning. Learning is the key to self actualization. The moment a child deviates from learning and focuses on fruits then, he/she is not able to move forward with full confidence.

Most of the times, it so happens that if our end become our means we are not working towards perfection. The purpose of life is not material gain, for nature never bestowed materialism on us. We all are born to enjoy the tunes of nature and strive towards knowing the secrets of nature.

As we grow big, we fail to dance to the tunes of Nature.

This is the revealing factor of Gita. Krishna says that we should rise above happiness and sorrow and learn to discover the secrets of Nature, learn to decipher our very purpose for coming on earth. Then only our journey of life would be completed.

Hence, the purpose of education should be self realization and not moving for selfish gains. When we crave for end results we do not give priority to the means and ways of reaching towards perfection and focus only on the end. Which might be not so good.

A hard work is noticed in every place and set up. No work gets unnoticed and it is only time factor which gives success. The satisfaction we drive from our work in itself is the reward we can get.

❑

Chapter-12

योगस्थः कुरु कर्माणि सङ्गत्यक्त्वा धनञ्जय।
सिद्धयसिद्धयोः समोभूत्वासमत्वं योग उच्यते।।

YOGASTAH KURU KARMAANI
SANGAM TYAKTVAA DHANANJAYA
SIDHI ASIDDHYO SAMOBHOOTVAA
SAMATVAM YOGA YUCHYATE

Aligned to self, work-full be
winner of wealth, attached not be,
Success or not same you be,
Equanimity is the right way, see!

अनाश्रितः कर्मफलं कार्यं कर्म करोति यः।
स संन्यासी च योगी च न निरग्निर्नचाक्रियः।।

In Gita, Krishna reveals to Arjuna that, Partha one does not become 'Yogi' or the enlightened one just by doing Karma or burning the sacred fire. One achieves the state of enlightenment by going through rigorous mental and physical planning and training. In Dhyanyoga, Krishna teaches Arjuna to have control over senses. A good and responsible teacher asks the student to become 'Ekagra' or concentrated. The focus and self discipline itself are the key to success and a start towards better performance. Many parents come to me saying that the school is not performing as per their wishes. Their child is not doing well. The school is at fault. They forget that the fault lies in the child itself. No child is weak or underperformer but the child is not focused toward education. The distractions of the outer world are forcing the child not to pay attention in class. A child will grasp the text only when he pays attention in class and enforcers the content taught in school, at home. Revision and re-revision of the work taught is of utmost importance.

The lord emphasizes that the karma should be done for their fulfillment and to realize the self and should not be directed reaping it's fruits on. Thus a complete realized soul is one which works not for self-fulfillment but for the larger society and he has achieved the status of a self realized one.

Every learner has come to this planet as a part of the greater super soul. Every learner has the spark of super soul and hence achieving that status of complete self potential realization is the purpose of education and the teacher motivates the learner towards it.

A good responsible teacher is one who does not take credit for the work and treats work as seva towards his learners. The process of doing work is joy and a good teacher does work to contribute, to set standards for his/her young learned.

A good teacher sees that the work which is being done is to improve the potentially of the learner and to support them in their improvement.

We all have come to this world to do work. The concept of 'Charaiveti' is mentioned in our religious text and it means 'keep on moving'. Becoming still is death. For when we work we utilize our time to the fullest and our energies are guided towards enhancing our ability and potentiality. A learner begins his life to achieve his/her innerself to the fullest and hence work assume a much more important magnitude.

A good teacher and a good institute is one where the abilities of its learners are guided towards achieving the best.

The achievement of perfection is divinity and our work assumes the status of divinity. We see that easy life, mobile, T.V.

enjoyment is accepted as part of upbringing to a learner. Our Shastras emphasize a tough, hard, disciplined life for even princes & princess. They have to go through tough training to face life later on. So hard work and religious training is part of growing up.

We see that parents come and talk about the marks of the students. They always complain that they are not satisfied with the marks. Marks are the ultimate goal of education. The child is many a time ridiculed to such an extent that he/she stops studying and runs away from studies. Studying and gaining knowledge is an enjoyable journey which should not be made arduous and boring.

Thus, rigorous mental and physical training at home and in school is the biggest preparation to face the challenges of life later on. No life is without tough competition and hurdle but a concentrated disciplined mind works towards success.

❑

Chapter-13

योगस्थः कुरु कर्माणि सङ्गत्यक्त्वा धनञ्जय।
सिद्धयसिद्धयोः समोभूत्वा समत्वं योग उच्यते।।

YOGASTHA KURU KARMAANI
SANGAM TYAKTVAA DHANANJAYA
SIDHI ASIDDHYO SAMOBHOOTVAA
SAMATVAM YOGA YUCHYATE

Aligned to self, work-full be
winner of wealth, attached not be,
Success or not same you be,
Equanimity is the right way, see!

Times like weather keeps on changing. Good times replace bad times and vice versa. Thus a teacher with years of experience and understanding that, unless and until he teaches his student to be equanimous in the changing scenario, he will not be able to do well in life. Being a part of nature we should be in equilibrium with self when tough conditions come. This weathering and deterioration could be stopped when our mental being has been enough prepared for hard times.

The learner at an impressionable state gets mentally disturbed and unfocussed. His energies gets wasted in trying to concentrate and lack of concentration leads to diversification and wastage of his talent.

In our culture, the yogic philosophy goes back to Lord Shiva and hence an able teacher guides his learner to achieve education through the complete alignment of body, self, mind and soul. When our total faculties, senses and energies are aligned towards the attainment of our goal, then we can achieve it easily. Shiva is the Adiguru a Sage who while living in the physical world is detached from the world. He is in a state of perpetual meditation and self conscious state. Thus, we have to train the young minds in such a way that they only focus on self and their energies within. Easily said but very difficult to achieve. This could only be achieved by the strong talented hand of an able guide.

The teaching in any case is a two way process, a transfer of knowledge from the learned to the learner and the acceptance of the knowledge of the learned by the learner.

A good teacher creates such an environment that, the learner is automatically guided towards the process of learning. For this, we have to give lots of good experiences at the learning stage to the young learner.

When our instinct, intuition, intelligence and insight becomes aligned, we do attain full success in our work. Then our work becomes inspirational and motivational to the peer group.

For a learner to get focused, first a teacher has to set exemplary standards. This world is full of distractions at all levels. There are physical, mental, emotional and intellectual distractions. A concentrated mind overcomes all these distractions and impurities and is able to rise above self and gain educational salvation.

Our extremely long Gurukul tradition boasts of mental alertness and concentration, an essential part of yogic accomplishment. For our learner in ancient times and the teachers of that bygone era, education at all levels was reaching the height of excellence. This was possible only through assigning a spiritual yogic value to the whole learning process. Education itself was a spiritual experience. In today's scenario, education has achieved a high commerce standard. We learn for job and tutors (Gurus) teach us for job. The tutors too get high remuneration for teaching students. Then what is school for?

In today's era, education is focused on commercial value and learning has become more an economical venture than a self satisfying process. Not many go to schools for complete accomplishment as a learner. This is where our Gita guides us to use all our energies and faculties without being deviated by external factors towards accomplishment of our goal. "Arise, awake and stop not till our goal is achieved."

This could only be achieved when our teacher sets such an example. A teacher should present before her learner without any addiction, desire or delusion for things which are non-materialistic.

A good responsible teacher tells the learner to accept success and failure; defeat and conquest in the same stride. Failure is the stepping stone to success and failure is the best teacher. We learn the most in the times of adversities but this is only possible if we do not accept defeat and get carried away with it. Defeat is like a marshy water which will pull us down. Only people with strong character rise above it.

Those learners who learn to handle defeat and failure and see into them as a teacher in disguise, rise to the levels they aspire to.

Many succumb to defeat and become restless, disturbed, weak and unable to focus, get into depressions and are not able to rise high in life.

This level of mental preparedness is achieved only in the custody of an able and serious teacher. A teacher who is himself able to handle failure can guide the student towards emotional freedom and ultimate success.

This is the basic sublime of Gita and it guides us that in all situations we should learn to handle our emotional status. The success should not carry us forward nor the failure deviate us from our path. In such a yogic situation of mental alertness and Ekagra (focused concentrated) we achieve Moksha or the ultimate level of mental freedom where our very purpose of life is achieved. The purpose is satisfaction and living life to its fullest than to achieve marks and jobs.

It is easier said than done. The very purpose of education should shift to the mental alertness of the learner and making him aware to his inner self and inner preparedness for all adversities of life. Our holy scriptures 'including Gita' speaks of the achievement of the inner alertness of the individual. It speaks of the movement of the sense organs inwardly to attain salvation. The educational salvation could be achieved by preparing the mental ground through discipline, hardwork, dedication, self study and the curiosity to know the unknown.

Thus, when a child is self disciplined, then the talent will be shown in all the spheres and he will be having an attitude of equanimity at times of difficulty.

❑

Chapter-14

बुद्धियुक्तो जहातीह उभे सुकृतदुष्कृते।
तस्माद्योगाय युज्यस्व योगः कर्मसु कौशलम्।।

BUDDHIYUKTO JAHAATEEHA
UBHE SUKRUTA DUSHKRUTE
TASMADHYOGAAYA YUJYASVA
YOGAH KARAMSU KASHALAM

Aligned to intellect a person leaves,
In the life good bad deeds,
Then align yourself in intellect way,
Skill in works is perfect way.

Education is a two way process in which through good communication skills, a teacher transcends his knowledge to the learner. In any classroom setting, it is the extreme intellect of a teacher which, through utmost care and skill is passed on to the student. We see that at young age parents request the teachers to give instructions they are unable to give. Students ralate more to teachers than parents.

In the process of teaching a learner benefits from the knowledge of the teacher and the teacher also keeps on upgrading the knowledge and communication skills.

All learners do not have same capacity of learning. This depends on the aptitude and intellect and interest of the learner for one particular subject. We see that each individual has one or more than one subject of his/her choice.

A good careful teacher uses all her thoughtfulness and intellect to see that the teaching process has been successfully completed and the learner has benefited from this two way process.

It is self-evident that our ancient religious texts which are testimony to those times speaks volume of illustrious Gurus like Vishwamitra, Dronacharya, Vashisht ,Valmiki and many like them. These Gurus meditated in hermitage and enhanced their teaching skills and their knowledge in such a way that they themselves benefited and their students benefited too. A good skillful teacher is one which can differentiate good from bad and is able to pass on this skill to the learner itself.

In the battlefield of Kurukshetra, Krishna transforms himself as the Guru of Arjuna and guides him to differentiate good from bad and enlighten his soul and intellect to a higher level platform. Krishna clears all the darkness surrounding Arjuna and skillfully guides him towards decision making. The basic concept of education is to enhance the potentiality of the learner and enlighten him in such a way that he is able to make proper decision in life. A good teacher helps the student gain confidence and understands the merit hidden within him.

A teacher just not finishes his task of teaching but goes a step further and removes all impurities lying within his student. He sees to it that student is chiseled in such a way that he has imbibed knowledge from the surroundings.

Thus, a skillful teacher is able to look beyond books and develop such a chord with his learner that the overall personality of the learner is skillfully moulded.

Krishna and Shiva were the yogic Gurus and there is ancient culture of yogic practices in our education system. Yoga is the enhancement of concentration and aligning one mind and soul. It sees to our mental and physical well-being. All Gurus land emphasis of meditation in our culture so that there is complete control over our minds. A controlled mind integrates all actions, feelings, thoughts and spirit.

This alignment of all the actions and positive reactions leads to a well developed personality and self-mastery.

The very purpose of education is to develop the right approach in an individual learner. The qualities of sincerity, honesty, dedication, hardwork and nobility are few of the virtues which could be taught by a teacher.

A good responsible teacher guides a student to be sincere. Sincerity is of thoughts and actions. A sincere learner knows what he is saying and says what he is doing. The sincerity in thoughts and in action takes a student on to path of development.

The virtue of dedication is doing what one feels and feels what one does. Unless and until we are dedicated on our path of learning, we cannot attain skillfulness and mastery in our craft. To reach to certain heights we have to be sincere in our endeavours and dedicated to the cause.

An honest learner is one who can think what he does and do what one thinks. Unless and until there is honesty in our purpose and goal we cannot achieve our success.

A responsible teacher guides a learner towards a sincere, dedicated honest purpose and lead the learner towards skillful accomplishment of his aims and objectives.

Objective of learning education is not only plain learning but going beyond it and realizing the self. Hence a good informed teacher slowly but successfully guides the learner towards self-realization of his own set of standards and thought processes.

The larger purpose of education is to benefit the society.

Thus, education always teaches nobility or benefitting the society in all possible ways.

Thus, a learned teacher sees to it that there is integrated, well kind approach towards education and this enhances the skillfulness and mastery of a learner. In my long course of teaching I have emphasized on swadhyay or learning for the self, one has to give calculated concentrated hours to learning to realize his own worth. Hard work is necessary for gaining information.

A good teacher just does not end his role with teaching but sees to the continuous growth of the learner.

❑

Chapter-15

दुःखेष्वनुद्विग्न मनाः सुखेषु विगतस्पृहः।
वीतरागभयक्रोधः स्थितधीर्मुनिरुच्यते।।

DUKHESHUANUDVIGNA MANAAH
SUKHESHU VIGATAH SPRUHA
VEETA RAAGA BHAYA KRODHAH
STHITADHEER MUNIRUCHYATE

Shakes not in grief when,
Concerned not in happiness when,
Leaves fear and anger attachment when,
Stable and Able he is called then.

These days depression and frustration are two things in learners which our modern education system and modern life style is breeding. The commercialization of education system coupled with job expectancy, education is adding fuel to these frustrations and depressions.

It is becoming very difficult for a learner to concentrate with so much of external pressures and disadvantages. This leads to disturbance in the mental equilibrium and peace of any student.

In yesteryears education was for proficiency in self but now the very basic purpose is getting desired jobs and students along with parents too are wanting job centre education and hence the child as a learner is unable to cope with it as the stakes are too high. Thus a balanced teacher could pass on equilibrium in a learner.

During the course of studies many a times the situation arises that a child is able to do good and many a times he fails in getting proficient. A stable teacher knows that learning is an ongoing process and during the course of learning one comes across many varied situations. The teacher is able to pacify both the parents and the student and convince them to remain in equilibrium during happiness and sorrow, failure and success.

A responsible teacher inculcates the value system in a learner that he/she does not get swayed or carried away by a disastrous situation.

The teacher is able to search solutions in time of need and sorrow and by giving appropriate solutions is able to help the learner come out of frustration and depression. In case of success the stable teacher is able to guide the learner to deal it with noble fortitude.

These days the growing trend amongst learner is the fear of failure and the insecurity of the future. The mental preparedness for the perspective harm in present or future has not been taught at the initial level. The examination pattern is such that it does not evaluate the potentiality of the learner and enhances it. The examination pattern only evaluates the preparedness for the exam. The portion prescribed is learnt but the overall text analysis is not done. So a learner only focuses on marks and not the content and hence loses out of life in the long run.

Fear of failure leads to anger and frustration. The frustration of hopelessness of situation and the happening of unplanned situation leads to a void and emptiness.

It is here that a responsible and balanced teacher steps in and takes the situation in his/her hand. It awakens in the learner the attitude to solve the problem.

The fear and anxiety will slowly disappear when a responsible teacher guides the learner towards practice and self-actualization.

When studies are done for realizing self and no other goal like (money, name and fame power) attached then slowly the fear vanishes and its place is taken up by peace and perfection.

Thus a balanced teacher practices equanimity and teaches the learner humility, forbearance and a state of equilibrium in studies and in all situations to which might arise in life later on.

❑

Chapter-16

या निशा सर्वभूतानां तस्यां जागर्ति संयमी।
यस्यां जाग्रति भूतानि सा निशा पश्यतो मुनेः।।

YAA NISHAA SARVA BHOOTHAANAAM
TASYAM JAAGARTI SAMYAMEE
YASYAAM JAGRUTI BHOOTHANI
SAA NISHAA PASHYATO MUNEH

What is darkness for living beings all,
That sees self controller, the knower of all,
In which is wakeful, living beings all,
sees, as darkness, thinker, knower of all.

When a learner leaves the security of the four walls of the home and enters the four walls of a premises called school, then parents entrust the future of their child into the hand of the Guru or the teacher. She is the learned one and the visionary and the one who guides the learner to evolve into a complete individual. It is the visionary midas touch of the Guru which takes a learner towards full realization.

Like Krishna, who could look beyond the Mahabharata war into the formation of a new world through the able hands of his follower, in the same way an able teacher looks beyond the present reality of the surrounding and forsees the future through his own eyes. He/she can differentiate between truth, fact and reality from the present appearances and carve out an entire new world for his learners and through his learners.

The prime target of any teacher is to see the spark in the child, encourage it and let it bloom to the fullest. This could only be done in the settings of school and through the able guidance of teachers. Parents are many a times blindfolded to the capabilities of their children and do not look beyond their expectations and into the dreams of their child.

Many a times it happens that parents want to live their dreams through their children but teacher's able guidance and an eye for valuing the potentiality of the child can help them grow into a good fully realized citizens. Thus a teacher has to act like a seer, a visionary, a transformer.

The Krishna in Mahabharata guides Arjuna to realize his capability and act with neutrality.

In the battlefield of Mahabharata, Arjuna succumbed to his thoughts and feelings on seeing the appearances at the battlefield. The vast encompass of army and the presence of his loved and learned ones made him weak and he fell into emotional turmoil. Krishna makes him rise from that emotional turbulence towards mental stability.

During the growing up years it so happens that the adolescent learner under the undue pressure of peers, parents and the exciting adventurous world falls into the well of emotional turbulence. It is at this time that the able hand of a visionary teacher pulls him out of emotional turbulence and guides him towards perfections.

An able visionary teacher looks beyond both weak and good students, dedicated and disillusioned ones too. Thus an able teacher overlooks the fault of weak students and mentors and guides them in such a way that they are able to understand their shortcomings and do better. In the same way an able teacher judges the nonapparent gaps of bright students and take them steps forward. For this a teacher has to change her/his own vision towards education in teaching students and go beyond the realm of reality and help the students thoroughly. A teacher should understand the responsibility that is thrust upon him and take up his role as a mentor seriously.

Whenever we go and look back into our lives we see and remember those teachers who have cast an influence on our lives. These are those very teachers who are always working long hours and are conscious to make a difference in the lives of learners and are alert to bring about positive changes in their learner's life. They become aware to the positive changes happening around them and use it to bring the change in their learner. They are always an asset to the institution and their student. Their own preparedness for life guides the students along the path of success.

❑

Chapter-17

विहाय कामान्यः सर्वान्पूमांश्चरति निःस्पृहः।
निर्ममो निरहङ्कारः स शान्तिमधिगच्छति।।

VIHAAYA KAAMAN YAH SARVAAN
PUMAAN CHARATI NISPRUHAH
NIRMAMO NIRAHANKAARAH
SA SHAANTIM ADHIGACHHATI.

All desires leaves one when,
As unannounced moves, one, when,
"Mine" and "I" removes one when,
Ultimate peace one gets then.

When a student leaves the four walls of the house and the confort zone of the parents and enters a new interactive world called school, then his first interaction is with his teacher, who is a pillar of strength in his life. In the course of my teaching experiences, I have found that some parents become very hostile and negative biased towards school. They fill their wards, mind with hatred and anxiety. Such learners are not able to absorb 100% from the school.

Hence, a teacher has to be an informed person who is capable of taking care of his students, life, and is able to mould his constant thought process, his emotions, his social interactions in such a way that there is everlasting positivity in the learner's mind.

The teacher has to rise above self, give up his ego, shed his own weaknesses and be in a position to take control of his learner's life. The ego of the Guru as "mine and me" has to sublime and in its place letting go of all his desires he has to accept his pupil in his fold and treat him like his own child.

The duty and responsibility of a teacher is of selfless service and to see to it that he is able to mould the desires of his learners through his constant positive actions and motivation towards the cherished goals.

A good teacher accepts all the learners as his own and takes them into his fold. He is not partial towards someone and shows total neutrality in action and deeds. He guides all the students with same vigor and strength and motivates them towards success. He does not get disheartened by the inefficiency of his students but act as a guiding pillar of strength.

Desires which are unfounded for and do not have a base, leads to attachment. Such attachments are most disastrous for mankind, desires lead to failures, defeats and sorrow. In Gita, Krishna is very explicit that every karma we do should be self less and nonbinding. The result of Karma is not in our hand, so attachment to karma should not exist.

Many a times during the parents-meet we find that a teacher knows more about the student than his/her immediate family. This is because of experience of handling so many students at the same time, a teacher develops the perception to decipher the inner individualistic traits of his learner.

An inspiring teacher is one which motivates the students towards learning. Inspite of realizing the reluctance of his learners, he motivates them to unbridle their inner potentialities and move ahead in life.

A teacher does not and should not differentiate students between good students and bad students. Teaching is a profession where we are unbiased towards our learners and treat all with equality and equanimity. A good teacher owns the responsibility of all his students and trains them such that they turn out to be achievers in life.

Teaching is not a profession but a passion and teacher is the carver of the destiny of so many people. Hence a good teacher should be respected by the learner from the bottom of his heart and the teacher slowly but firmly mould the capabilities of his/her learners. He teaches them in such a way that they move towards betterment.

A school should be an environment where a uniform culture of brotherhood is developed. A good teacher cuts the bondage of selfish 'Me' and ties it to a uniform 'Us'. It develops a culture of a good team and leads the team to success.

❑

Chapter-18

लोकेऽस्मिन्द्विविधा निष्ठा पुरा प्रोक्ता मयानघ।
ज्ञानयोगेन साङ्ख्यानां कर्मयोगेन योगिनाम्।।

LOKESMINDVIVIDHAA NISHTAA
PURAA PROKTAA MAYAANAGHA
GNAANA YOGENA SANKHYAANAAM
KARMAYOGENA YOGINAAM

For this world, in ancient times,
By me shown were, paths, two kinds,
For seekers of self, the knowledge path,
For endeavouring ones, the action path.

Teaching is one of the most difficult professions. A profession where a child as a learner looks up to the teacher and initiates and defines his value systems. A learner shows keen interest in the ability of the teacher. Hence a good teacher is one who is knowledgeable about his own education and has self-worth.

A good teacher is able to show his knowledge through his actions and deeds. These actions are observed by a keen learner. There are many teachers who have a good knowledge bank but are unable to disseminate the knowledge amongst their learners either for want of expertise, requisite talent, shyness or fear. Thus action and knowledge by a good teacher is a prerequisite to teaching keeping the knowledge to self and refraining from passing it on to the learner is not being true to our profession.

As the civilization grew and became more advance the man moved from the ability to use his/her own hands to the capacity to acquire language, communicate to the other person, initially through sign languages and then through verbal communication. Slowly as man evolved, he developed the skills to use his thought and imagination into proper words and language.

The evolution of the mankind is the evolution of the ability to acquire more and more information from the surroundings. This knowledge creates a bigger awareness and a good teacher is one who possesses enough information about the concerned subject to be taught.

The lessons and experiences learnt in the past and comprehension and proper undertaking of the present and the ability to be fully prepared for the future is, what makes a good teacher.

The Krishna in Mahabharata, while giving discourses to Arjuna at the battlefield says, that our ancient text has advised Gyana marg and Karmayogi marg for its achievers. Gyana marg is one where a seeker wants to contemplate the higher order of awareness and move his sensory organs inwards to achieve knowledge. Karmayogi marg or the path of action is for the outward seekers. These are the people who want to perform and stay attached to the world through their actions. A good teacher like Krishna helps the learners to decipher which path the learners want to take—the Gyana marg or the Karmayogi marg.

The Gyana marg or the path of knowledge is for thinkers, philosphers, researchers, who want to delve into the higher streams of awakening and create something knew or share their knowledge further. Like our yesteryear yogis, they can work on the cause effect linkages. The present day scientists are like yogis of the earlier times and they reason out to carve out a path for others to follow. They search for optional ways to achieve the target and a good efficient teacher is able to help such learners to awaken their inner light and reach the path of enlightenment.

Not all students or learners have the dedication and patience to adopt the Gyana marg. Most of the learners want to follow the path of actions or Karma. Hence their skills and knowledge have to be enhanced in such a way that can lead their lives as doers.

The doers can learn and develop adequate skills and are able to carry out their path in an efficient and practical way.

All the learners look up to their teachers and hence a teacher following the Gyana marg becomes one who is the inspirer. With the abundance of knowledge the true seeker, a knower of all educational inputs, a seer becomes a guiding force for all its students.

The teacher who motivates the students for the concentration of skills and helps in developing expertise in the action path, is an accomplisher and achiever.

Education is not only achieving more knowledge but knowledge could be acquired by lot of methods including exercise, experimentation, practical, projects, games, assignments, artistic and scientific undertakings.

The responsible teacher sees that along with the gaining of knowledge, a student is awakened to the inner self and starts contemplating and analyzing the work given and starts creative and logical thinking to achieve results.

A good responsible teacher has the ability to analyze the potentiality of his/her learner and find out the orientation of the learner and motivate him accordingly.

An informed teacher helps in building up nation by inculcating in the learner the awareness to infuse the accumulated knowledge into the creative logical analysis for a better nation. Unless and until a learner learns to be critical, analyze knowledge and channelize it towards creativity much success would not be achieved.

The perspective towards education has to be changed. Education should appear as a puzzle to be solved, a theory to be deciphered, an invention to be made. Education is not planned accumulation of date but the interpretation of available data for new concepts to be decoded. Here an informed teacher comes in handy as a guiding principle in learner's life.

❑

Chapter-19

देवान्भावयतानेन ते देवा भावयन्तु वः।
परस्परं भावयन्तः श्रेयः परमावाप्स्यथ।।

DEVAANBHAAVAYATAANENA
TE DEVAA BHAAVAYANTU VAH
PARSPARAM BHAAVAYANTAH
SHREYAH PARAMAVAAPSYATHA

Let the divine wish you well,
Let you wish divine well,
Mutually wish you each other well,
Reap then best and you progress well.

The basic purpose of teaching is the overall growth of the learner and this is achieved well when there is a creative and well balanced assemblage of parents, teachers and the learners.

Unless and until teachers and learners share a good bondage of understanding, an overall growth of the learner is nonetheless impossible.

Learning at school level is not possible in a good way for learner till there is a proper coordination of the teacher and the student. Thus, a good teacher understands this diction and knows the importance of mutual acceptance. The teacher who knows that only when there is mutual trust and cooperation from both sides would learning be made easy and it will develop into a two way process. Overall progress of the learner is possible only with the mutual trust, confidence and caring of all the components. (Like the school, teacher, parents and learner and their proper involvements in the growth process.) The care the teacher showers on the learner goes a long way in making difference in the learning process and benefiting the learners.

A good teacher not only shares the success of a learner but also shares the weakness, shortcomings, failures, frustrations and drawbacks of the learner and gets them converted into a path of growth. A good teacher helps the students to identify his negative thoughts and convert it into positive actions.

At the learner stage, his success is best identified as the achievement of Guru. A good teacher not only feels elated but immensely satisfied at the success achieved by his learner for he sees the fulfillment of his teachings and hardwork. The mutual trust and understandings when the Guru is the giver and the learner is the receiver who is receiving and both are happy at the rise of the learner and that is the most inspiring stage.

Swami Ramakrishna Paramahansa is known by the intellectual achievement of his Shishya—Vivekanand. The mutual glorification of the teaching of Ramakrishna and complete adaption of them in real life and their spread led to the divine success of the learning process and the elevated Guru Shishya Parampara.

Thus we see that illustrious Shishya add to the glory of the Guru and both rise simultaneously in this process. The teachers and learners both include all the intervening groups in their progress. The progress and growth of the Shishya becomes the only motive of the Guru and it leads to the emotional growth and development of the Shishya.

Thus we see that when the Guru is an elevated one, then Shishya also rises from the status of a mere learner and for his learning becomes a divine experience and it is a mutual exchange of learning given at one end and received at another end.

When learning is a divine process then all the components involved in the process wish each other well and their basic objective becomes an all round growth of the learner.

The atmospheres all around is that of awakening and the spirit of give and take is the cardinal point of this exchange.

Our culture, as it reflects from different texts, revels that education has always been accorded a spiritual status. The hermitage of the Guru was the learning ground and Gurumata the mentor and caretaker. The atmosphere at hermitage was of divine revelation for all.

Same Guru-Shishya parampara needs to be reawakened for the society to progress at large.

❑

Chapter-20

यद्यदाचरति श्रेष्ठस्तत्तदेवेतरो जनः।
स यत्प्रमाणं कुरुते लोकस्तदनुवर्तते।।

YADYADAA CHARATI SHRESHTAH
TATTADEVETARO JANAH
SA YAT PRAMAANAM KURUTE
LOKASTAD ANUVARTATE

How behaves the best of men
So behaves the rest of men
His example, they will show
Saying "He did so! so we do so!!".

Teaching is one process where a learner imitates the teacher. Thus the conduct and value system set up by the teacher is a guiding principle for the learner. The teacher becomes a role model for not only the learner but the fellow teachers, parents and colleagues too.

The teacher becomes like a pathfinder, a trend breaker and his conduct a benchmark for the others to follow. If the teacher indulges in malpractices and bad habits, then the student also imitates those habits.

A hardworking, disciplined, well-oriented teacher is an ideal for his learner. This is one service where as a human resource the learner from the beginning starts eulogizing the teacher.

At a very nascent stage, the learner agrees more to the dictates of the teacher than even of the parents and guardians. So in order to be a leader, a teacher has to practice regularly to move towards a better and developed cult, a real hero for the young impressionable mind.

A teacher is one which influences generations of a country. The complete thought process is the making of a good capable teacher. In the same way a bad teacher spoils the mindset of the youth and the learner.

If a teacher is well behaved, disciplined, hardworking, truthful and dedicated towards his students, then the learners reciprocate by love, respect, warm wishes towards the teachers. They also imbibe good moral values from the teacher and it helps in building sound moral characters. The character and the value system is the most important thing which a good teacher can pass on to its learner.

This is one profession which is more of a passion and it is the extreme form of social service where the teacher passes on all he has in the form of talent, potentiality and value system to his/her pupils.

Thus, this is a challenge which a teacher takes up on himself, the role and responsibility for his learners. We read in our ancient texts that Rama went to Swayamvar of Sita with his brother and Guru and there the culmination of his marriage to Sita took place. Hence in yesteryears Gurus, had a deep influence in the personal lives of learners and commanded a respect more than that of the parents.

Not only in primary classes but, even higher up the learners imitate the conduct of their teachers. They are observant of the behavior, approach, interaction of the teachers and follow suit.

The young minds could be guided in the right direction only if we have teachers with right conduct and hence the responsibility on the teacher increases manifold. A teacher is reshaping the future generations of the country so we should have such teachers who can influence young minds in a constructive right direction.

Thus, to see that the future of a country is secured, we should have right minded teachers.

Chanakya was a Guru who shaped the destiny of our country for times to come. He created history where the cause of the nation got reshaped for generations to come.

Hence the importance of good teachers at no time should be a debatable topic.

❑

Chapter-21

न मे पार्थास्ति कर्तव्यं त्रिषु लोकेषु किञ्चन।
नानवाप्तमवाप्तव्यं वर्त एव च कर्मणि।।

NA ME PAARTHAASTI KARTAVYAM
TRISHU LOKESHU KINCHANA
NAANAVAAPTAMAVAAPTVYAM
VARTA EVA CHA KARMANI

Partha! For me in three worlds,
There are no pending works,
None to attain and none to do,
Still the work I always do.

In universe (the creation of Lord Krishna) is such that everything is moving and is in a constant state of work. The concept of 'charaveti' or keep moving is applicable to the Universe.

The same is communicated by the Lord that, though he has achieved everything and the whole universe is in his control still, he is following the principle of hard work. Still the Lord respects work.

So a Guru, as a human impersonification of God, should give utmost importance to work and should set work as a role model for the students to imitate. We can not do away with work. It is the only medium through which a teacher can guide and motivate a young learner towards discharging one's duty.

There is absolutely no substitute for good effective work.

In the Brahmand (Universe) everything is doing work at the constant standard set by the laws of nature. Earth is moving without stopping, moon and sun are in a constant state of work and so is even the tiniest of creature. Work is the fundamental guiding principle of the Universe and should be adequately imitated by the human being.

Work is worship, goes the English diction and so is rightly prophesied by the Gita—Karma is the Cardinal Principle of this holy text. This holy text guides us to do the rightful, just work and choose the righteous path.

Most of us grow up thinking that we have to perform a certain responsibility as duty. When our obligations and responsibility become mere duty then our work ceases to be worship.

In Gita it is strongly mentioned that, our work is worship and this prayer could only be achieved when all our faculties are trained and channelized towards accepting our duty as a prayer. When duty becomes sewa or service we have attained the maximum height of spiritual divine state and it helps us to move further on the spiritual path.

Teaching is supposed to be one of the most difficult professions. Apart from the quality of teacher and his educational qualification her/his behavior and attitude too influences the learning ability of learner.

A teacher who is well behaved, meticulous, disciplined and focuses on her/his internal improvement, is able to guide the learner in a much better way and sees to her personal growth too.

Thus we should see that as a teacher it does not become our profession but passion to guide young, impressionable minds and influence their destiny through our conduct and hard work.

A teacher need not be told of her duties but should be one who adopts duty as a selfless service. When a teacher rises above self and performs exemplary work then he is able to guide the learner towards perfection.

❑

Chapter-22

न बुद्धिभेदं जनयेदज्ञानां कर्मसङ्गिनाम्।
जोषयेत्सर्वकर्माणि विद्वान्युक्तः समाचरन्।।

NA BUDDHI BHEDHAM JANAYED
AGYAANAM KARMASANGINAAM
JOSHAYET SARVA KARMAANI
VIDWAAN YUKTAH SAMAACHARAN

Do not disturb the ignorant one,
Who does the work with attachment,
Can show him the way the intelligent one,
By doing well with detachment.

A good detached teacher is one who considers teaching a passion and a part of selfless work where they are shaping the future of the entire generations without a thought of reaping the fruits of the work.

The great teacher like Socrates, Parshuram, Vasistha, Vishwamitra, Sandipani, Ramakrishna Paramahansa worked hard in imparting education to their Shishyas and seeing to it that the learner rose in life.

Education is the noblest of professions for in this profession one only learns to give and finds pleasure in giving.

Many a times students and learners do not even come back with adequate respect for the teacher but still the teacher is happy seeing the student rise. Thus this selfless service given by the teacher should be imitated in the society and especially by the learners in their life.

The dedication, commitment, hard work and seriousness, that is imitated by the teacher to bring out the best in a student should become the guiding principle in the lives of learners.

For example, take the situation at the kurukshetra before the beginning of the Mahabharata. It was the guiding speech by our very own Guru, Krishna, which cleared all the doubts from the mind of his Shishya and led him to glory.

Thus, in no way a Guru has any lust to gain over or get rewards from the growth of their Shishyas.

Still, there are few Gurus like, Dronacharya which see their growth in the growth of their learners and become biased. Dronacharya become a biased Guru and in favour of his Shishya Arjuna brought harm to his Shishya Eklavya. The history is testimony to it that Dronacharya lost his life because of his learned Shishya, the Arjuna, in the battlefield of Mahabharata.

This we see that seeing the nobility and depth of this profession. Teaching is a selfless work which becomes contribution and a detached service and the Guru is ready to share the fruits of his knowledge amongst his learners.

A teacher is supposed to be all encompassing, sharing and caring for his loved ones—the learners and always be conscious for their growth and well-being.

Thus, seeing the example of Dronacharya a teacher should learn that it has to see the growth of even the ignorant and not only dedicated learners and bring about their growth. A teacher should rise above biases and personal shortcoming and should not develop favouritism for his learners and get all of them grow in glory.

A good teacher through gentle persuasion brings about positive changes in the learner.

A learner thus stands as a good replica of its Guru and brings him an everlasting glory and success in this life and in life hereafter.

❑

Chapter-23

इन्द्रियाणि पराण्याहुरिन्द्रियेभ्यः परं मनः ।
मनसस्तु परा बुद्धिर्योबुद्धेः परतस्तु सः ।।

INDRIYAANI PARAANYAHU
INDRIYEBHYAH PARAM MANAH
MANASASTU PARAA BUDDHIH
YO BUḊDHEH PARATASTU SAH

Organs, it is said, are much great,
More than organs mind is great,
More than mind, intellect great,
Greater than intellect is spirit ultimate.

For a responsible teacher school and teaching are not commercial venture. They take it as a passionate profession and gets attached with the learner. The humanly touch to teaching influences the EQ of the child and motivates and directs him/her towards learning thus when a learner gets motivated he/she has warm and positive feelings towards learning and the teacher.

This further guides the learner towards dedicated concentrated action.

When learning becomes a focused, dedicated selfless act, then learner is able to grasp knowledge better and is able to rise more.

When a learner has warm feelings for learning, then his emotional status is at equilibrium and he has good thoughts which finally gets converted into concentrated actions.

In today's scenario, we see and feel that many children feel left out in the education system inspite of their intellect and dedication. They feel deprived and unmotivated in the educational system. They also feel insulted by their teachers and peer group and this hampers their learning and the marks.

We see that many students are further rebuked by the teachers in the classes. This brings in them a sense of inferiority complex and harms their confidence.

Thus, a responsible teacher is one which believes in righteous actions and knows that healthy body and focused mind can do wonders.

A dedicated teacher knows that almost all the success lies in a disciplined mind and mind is the source of creativity. This creativity leads to miraculous actions and bringing about good changes in the society.

A good teacher always believe that an inspiration is the key to positive action. As the saying goes success is 99% perspiration and 1% inspiration. Hence a good teacher guides the student to perspire and achieve good results.

A good teacher ignites the light inside the learner and motivate him to move towards success.

❑

Chapter-24

यदा यदा हि धर्मस्य ग्लानिर्भवति भारत।
अभ्युत्थानमधर्मस्य तदात्मानं सृजाम्यहम्।।

YADAA YADAA HI DHARMASYA
GLAANIR BHAVATI BHAARATA
ABHYUTTHAANAM ADHARMASYA
TADAATMAANAM SRUJAAMYAHAM

Whenever whenever the right is harmed,
Whenever whenever the wrong has formed
When wrong is up and right is down,
Then Bharata I come on my own.

There was lot of confusion all around and the battlefield was all set. The fight had to begin and Arjuna lay confused as what the course of action should be for him.

Krishna rose from the chariot and spoke the discourse to remove the confusion in the mind of his Shishya.

Same happens with a good teacher. A good teacher is more awakened, enlightened and aware of his surroundings, duties, responsibilities and hence is able to guide the learner towards enlighten.

In life, it so happens that many a times, there is chaos and confusion in life. A good teacher teaches the student to come out of that life with flying colours like Krishna did during Mahabharata war.

The training and guidance, which is given to deal with at the time of confusion, helps the learner to overcome difficulties and depressing situation.

A good teacher produces leader capable of handling tough situations and taking responsibility in life.

Life is not all about rosy situations and education is not all about academics. The very purpose of education is to teach the learner the basic life skills which come in very handy at the time of dealing difficult situations.

A good teacher knows the responsibility and awakens the learner towards life skills.

A responsible teacher teaches the learner to think, crede, innovate and produce results. A learner, who is able to think, can handle any difficult situation later on in life without getting destroyed and disinclined.

❑

Chapter-25

परित्राणाय साधूनां विनाशाय च दुष्कृताम्।
धर्मसंस्थापनार्थाय संभवामि युगे युगे।।

PARITRAANAAYA SASDHUNAM
VINAASHAYACHA DUSHKRUTAAM
DHARMA SAMSTHAAPANAARTHAYA
SAMBHAVAAMI YUGE YUGE.

To protect the good and right of men,
To destroy the evil and wrong of men,
To establish right at each stage,
I occur at right time, age by age.

The basic purpose of education is development of a sound character in the learner. A good moral learner is an asset for the system and this is basically the very foundation of education.

To achieve this, a good teacher lays emphasis on right practices, method and values and inculcates them in the learner. He himself sets a role model and sees to it that it is imitated by the learner.

A good teacher keeps an eye on that good practices are not deteriorating and good system is not becoming inefficient. He keeps a check on wrong practices and keeps a check and balance/ system and sees to it that his learner imbibes right practices and value system.

Sri Krishna as an embodiment of Guru says that he takes birth and rebirth to see that the might of right is established. And to do this he is ever conscious.

At the time when Arjuna was confused and did not know which path to follow—Krishna rose and awakened the positive feeling in Arjuna and took him to the path of righteousness. In the same way a teacher takes upon himself the role of a leader and the responsibility to remove all evil practices and establish right practices in the society through his learners.

A moral society would be established only when all its citizens are people of sound character. A just society very soon move on to the path of development and creativity.

Karma should not be done with a desire to gain benefits. It should be Nishkam Karma—one without any self-interest and then only it reaps proper dividends.

Education is not just a statistic. It is a process where a good teacher guides the students to contemplate and do research. A good teacher guides the students to think and recreate. When the thinking process in the students is awakened and they move on to the higher realm of knowledge them the learner's mind is open to new awakenings and wisdom. This helps the students to be more creative and the results are more fruitful and constructive.

❑

Conclusion

Self study or swadhyay is what is the education all about. If a learner does not get into the habit of swadhyay then he will not realize his potentiality and inner worth.

Swadhyay means devoting time to learning, contemplating, realizing self-worth and opening up to new realms of understanding. This is possible only when one opens up to inner-self and closes all the doors of outward distraction at bay.

Swadhyay requires sacrifice of material desires, of longings, and makes the learner focus towards an aim or good in life.

A good responsible teacher helps the students identify his goal of life and move towards it with unidirectional commitment.

It is not easy for a young learner to get into the practice of swadhyay for it requires lot of patience, commitment and a strong will and to be free from all distractions and diversions. Since the learner is too young hence, getting involved in wrong company is very easy and it is here that a seasoned teacher guides and motivates the learner towards self sacrifice and get focused.

Self improvement is possible only through self study.

These days, tuition industry is in vogue and has arisen parallel to the education system. In fact, kids as young as montessori are getting private tuitions. Parents in the guise of shelving their burden have hired a person to take care of their child's education. This is costing young learner a lot. They need a parallel support system to assist them in education. They cannot learn and focus on their own.

A good teacher is one who helps the students understand the text and contemplate on it, reason it, solve it and invent new theories. This is possible only through self-study.

When one does self-study, then he actualizes his weaknesses and strengths. Thus, self-study is the only way to realizing the full potential of a learner and paves the way for his self actualization and inner growth.

❑

Inference

The basic purpose of learning for everyone is enhancement of knowledge, improvement in personality and overall development of the learner. This is possible only when the teacher and the learner go hand in hand to utilize their all available resources.

In our schools most of the times parents come complaining that they pay fees to the school system but their ward is not doing well. They put all the blame on school and curse the teacher for not bringing about the desired result in their child. They feel that their responsibility gets over by putting the blame on the teacher and passing on the buck to the other person. They fail to understand that it is giving time to their child which is of utmost importance in bringing about the change. I tell the mother to just sit with their young child and encourage him/her to study. The positive inclination of the parents especially the mother goes a long way in bringing about the desired changes in the child.

When the parents are interested towards overall development of their child then the child also shows keen devotion for studying and waits to have self enhancement. A young child is like a spore if given care and utmost devotion blooms into a beautiful flower, if neglected grows wild and depressed.

Even a good teacher showers all his care and attention to the child as a learner and focus on the overall development of the child.

A good responsible learner imbibes the knowledge and grows into a knowledgeable centre and grows as an asset for the school, family and society as a whole.

A good learner grows as an attribute to the society, guiding and focusing it to improve further. Thus the role of the teacher is very important. It sees that learner grows as an informed citizen and this citizen contributes back to the society.

Thus if we want to build a society, then we should build schools as institution and not as commercial venture.

Teaching as it is, is one of the noblest professions and its award is the growth of society, this is possible by enhancing the personality of its learner by all the endeavors put in by its teacher.

Thus, a responsible teacher through all its knowledge and skills, add to the betterment of the society.

❑

Orientation

In education unless and until the learner is aware and wanting to learn, no amount of good teacher could teach him. A student has to be an awakened learner, one who is open to ideas, visions, and keen to learning. For only then a good teacher is required who is ready to teach such learners who have an eye on getting trained. How could any one train a person which is refusing to getting trained?

Thus teaching becomes a two way process—a keen learner and a focused teacher. A good learner is able to grasp knowledge from whichever source it is available. A good learner is able to hunt for the Guru For example: Vivekanand and Ramakrishna Paramahansha. Our religious text as testimony to ancient times, speak of a rich cultural lineage of Guru-Shishya Parampara.

In such a divine situation where the transmission of knowledge is divinity the teacher rises to the plank of the ultimate master—the divine creator and Shishya becomes the ultimate receiver—the seed of creation.

In our school set-up, we see that though the teacher is capable but all the students are not able to receive from them in the same way. This is because both teacher and student needs to possess certain qualities for the transformation to occur in a good way. When both the learner and the teacher possess adequate qualities then is the learning process an effective one and it is an enriching experience for the giver and the receiver.

A teacher needs to be knowledgeable in his subject. For whatever knowledge a teacher possess, the same he is able to transmit to his student. If the teacher is knowledgeable, then he is able to clear those concepts of his students/learners. Knowledge without experience is useless. For many a times the teacher possess extreme knowledge but is not able to disseminate it to his learners.

Good concept clearing is only possible through good experiences. Profound experience enhances the knowledge skill and the efficiency of the teacher to pass it on to his learner.

It is also a common day observation in classes that many a times the teacher has expertise, experience but is not confident enough to pass on the knowledge base to his learners. His communicative skill should be such that he is able to disseminate the information correctly to the learner.

Thus, we see that it is very important that the teacher is the potent source of strength and capability and an inspiration for his learner.

It is a common day observation that many a times the learner fails to have respect for the teacher. They are arrogant and treat their Guru in dark shade. Their parents are ever complaining and demeaning the teacher in poor light. Thus, if a learner is awakened and is serious about gathering information from the teacher, then he should learn to hold his teacher at high pedestal. Worshipping and respecting the teacher helps the teacher in loving the child and seeing to his proper growth.

The learner should have respect for the teacher and should be in a position to serve him.

In yesteryears, we use to see that learners used to go to Gurukul and serve their master and their wife. They used to treat the wife as Gurumata and served the Guru well. They used to do all the household work and served their masters well and gained knowledge.

This framework has gone but still the reverence for the Guru is the prime duty for a learner to imbibe knowledge.

A learner who is not curious is not able to rationalize the various aspects of universe. Thus an inquisitive mind is a must if a learner has to learn and understand new facts and concepts.

Thus, in this environment the Guru and the Shishya get linked by a unique bond of energy transfer. The energy in the form of knowledge flows from the Guru to the Shishya, and leads the Shishya to a higher plank of enlightenment.

The strong foundation of society is good education. Only when education is embraced with utmost reverence, we can envision the future of our nation, soaring to new heights.

Depression and anxiety are natural in a human being but these malice can be removed by reviving our old cultures, reliving with our good and intellectual past with its glory. Our scriptures and their interpretation emphasize the development of strong individuals with solid character and personality, who are not easily swayed by materialistic success and gains. The outer world should not be able to lead them astray. They should be content and happy within themselves and their happiness should lie in strong and sturdy foundation of the society and well defined in their childhood.

The very purpose of education is character building and serving our society, family and the Nation.

This part of education should be envisaged again to have fearless individuals who can work towards making the society a better place to live.

❑